The People Measurement Manual

The People Measurement Manual

Measuring Attitudes, Behaviours and Beliefs in Your Organization

DAVID WEALLEANS

GOWER

Published by
Gower Publishing Limited
Gower House
Croft Road
Aldershot
Hants GU11 3HR
England

Gower Publishing Company
Suite 420
101 Cherry Street
Burlington, VT 05401-4405
USA

David Wealleans has asserted his right under the Copyright, Designs and Patents Act 1988 to be identified as the author of this work.

British Library Cataloguing in Publication Data
Wealleans, David
   The people measurement manual: measuring attitudes,
   behaviours and beliefs in your organization
   1. Employees – Attitudes 2. Work measurement
   I. Title
   658.3'1

   ISBN 0 566 08380 9

Library of Congress Cataloging-in-Publication Data
Wealleans, David.
   The people measurement manual: measuring attitudes, behaviours and beliefs in your
   organization / David Wealleans.
      p. cm.
   Includes index.
   ISBN 0-566-08380-9 (alk. paper)
     1. Consumer satisfaction–Evaluation. 2. Job satisfaction–Evaluation. 3.
   Organizational effectiveness–Evaluation. I. Title.

HF5415.335.W425 2003
658.8'12–dc21   2002027160

Typeset by IML Typographers, Birkenhead, Merseyside and printed in Great Britain by TJ International Ltd, Padstow, Cornwall.

Contents

List of Figures and Tables   vii

Preface   ix

1   The Need to Measure   **1**
People make us competitive – The pace of change – Knowing where we are –
Customer expectations – Knowing our strategies and objectives – Dealing with
uncertainty – Operational versus strategic measurement – A company with
potential – Summary

2   Understanding People   **11**
The importance of people – 'It's not personal' – Taking account of people – Aspects
of human contribution – Personal and organizational input – Determining key success
factors – Identifying primary   concerns – Pinning it down – Intuition versus objectivity –
Summary

3   Creating the Right Conditions   **24**
Using objectivity – The need to retain feelings and impressions – Understanding
individuality – Coping with diversity – Using impressions constructively –
Justifying conclusions – Removing doubt and suspicion – Openness and integrity –
Summary

4   Choosing the Measurements   **34**
What to measure – The benefits of good selection – Behaviours – Behavioural links –
Effects on processes – Links to other measurements – Strategic versus operational
levels – Observer effects – Measurement criteria – Summary

5   Human Measurement Techniques   **45**
The uncertainty of measuring people – Gaining objectivity – Using evaluation criteria –
Techniques of measurement – Objectives and results – Direct and indirect indicators –
Quantification – Pitfalls – Summary

6   Employee Surveys   **59**
The use of employee surveys – Question design – Gap identification – Application and
coverage – Promoting the usage – Running a survey – Analysing the results – Summary

7   Measurement by Interview   **76**
The interview technique – Planning an interview programme – Timing – Questions –
Conducting the interview – Analysing the results – Strengths and weaknesses –
Summary

8 **Monitoring People** 94

The continuous measurement technique – Designing the system – Planning and preparation – Taking the measurements – Analysis – Reporting – Reviewing the system – Summary

9 **Analysis and Action** 107

Introduction – Analysis personnel – Baselining – Comparative and absolute targets – Identifying areas for action – Action planning – Monitoring and follow-up – Summary

10 **Understanding and Using the Environment** 125

Introduction – The short and long term – Tracking environmental factors – Lagging and leading indicators – Rate of change – Trends and blips – Dealing with individual deviations – Summary

11 **Keeping It Going** 136

Introduction – Objectivity – Creating rigour – Constancy of purpose – Combining with other programmes – Maintaining the momentum – Summary

Index 145

List of Figures and Tables

FIGURES

1.1	The measurement continuum	9
2.1	Task importance and urgency	21
5.1	Target indication	55
6.1	Barchart of all reported values	70
6.2	Normal distribution	71
7.1	Interview response chart	91
9.1	Measurement analysis by champion and team	109
9.2	Consistent failure to achieve target	116
9.3	Highly variable results	117
9.4	Worsening trends	118
9.5	Measurement 'blips'	118

TABLES

2.1	Samples for mean and range calculations	14
3.1	Measurement results with means and ranges	30
5.1	Quantifying the measurement scale	47
5.2	Measurement scale criteria	48
5.3	Example measurements on a simple scale	54
6.1	Situation and importance answers	63
6.2	Normal distribution coverage	72
6.3	Individual survey response summary	72
7.1	Report of interview data	91
8.1	Measurement method examples	100
9.1	Disadvantages of separate baselining surveys	110
10.1	Chi-squared distribution	134

Preface

Most business measurements directly consider factors that are obviously quantifiable. These include, for instance, financial data and general quality performance statistics. Shortly after I had finished writing *The Organizational Measurement Manual*, the publishers asked me whether I had ever considered writing about the softer side of measurements, specifically those related to people working within an organization, since they had perceived a need for greater information on the subject.

In my working life I have always tried to ensure that the people factors in any project rank as high as the technical ones. I have also both created and supported a number of initiatives that aim to put figures to how people feel, act and behave. A little more research into the subject then produced this book, whose purpose is to be a general guide to managers and businesspeople that will allow them to manage their own people measurement initiatives.

We all know that dealing with people well can be one of the main success factors for a business, yet it is extremely hard to pin down; it is far easier to find and eliminate a bug from a large, distributed software system than it is to tackle low morale or political tensions in the workplace. I hope that this book helps you create a systematic approach to understanding the people issues in your own organization.

DAVID WEALLEANS

CHAPTER ONE

The Need to Measure

PEOPLE MAKE US COMPETITIVE

People are at the heart of any competitive strategy. No matter how technical or automated our operations, at some point they still rely on human beings to make the enterprise a success. It follows that creating success relies on making the best use of the people that drive our organization. Competition, which provides an impetus for every type of organization in one form or another, whether profit-making or not, requires us not only to employ techniques that strive to make the best use of our people, but also to continually evaluate how well they are doing so that we may keep adjusting and improving our approach.

THE NEED TO COMPETE

It almost seems unnecessary to open a book by stating that we need to compete. After all, every commercial enterprise has always had to do battle with others that are seeking the same customers. But we do this to emphasize how hard we have to compete in the business environment of the twenty-first century. Every organization is continually finding ways of making itself more attractive to customers, so each competing business has to be equally aggressive just to stay in the race.

This competitive process is now more fast-paced than ever. At one time, companies could look forward to long years of stability; they produced products that would have an extended life and customers who would stay loyal and constant indefinitely. Today, products seem to fade and lose their attraction as rapidly as a bunch of flowers: customers buy from whom they acquire the best deal, regardless of past relationships; competitors deliberately steal our markets and a multitude of external pressures prevent us from keeping anything the same for any length of time.

In manufacturing, the pace of change has been particularly noticeable, probably because we can look back to days when things were more stable. One of the key contributors to this has been the adoption of fast product 'churn', pioneered by many Japanese electronics companies. Fast churn is an approach whereby new product models are launched very rapidly, often replacing old versions after they have been on the market for less than a year. This has substantially replaced the old philosophy of keeping the product on the market until the point where it loses its attraction to customers in order to maximize return on the development effort. Churned products are replaced by others with slightly enhanced features, functions or styling even though there is still nothing 'wrong' with the superseded model. A good example of this strategy can be seen in the Japanese motorcycle industry which is renowned for having beaten its competitors by producing new models at a staggering pace, even though motorcycle technology does not really advance that quickly (compared to, for example, developments in integrated circuits or genetic science) and new models are just repackaged versions of existing technology. This fast churn by some companies creates an increased demand for products (as many buyers are highly motivated to dispose of yesterday's products and buy the latest edition) and elevates customer expectations, forcing other companies to try to adopt the same, or even better, churn rates. The phenomenon of churn has itself been encouraged by today's emphasis on increased customer choice; people are no longer prepared to queue for standard off-the-shelf items and services

– they expect to have a choice and to have any irritations that they find in current offerings corrected in tomorrow's products.

While this incredible rate of change has been most evident in manufacturing and computer and communications technology, there are also plenty of examples from the service industries. We could, for instance, look at Internet service provision, where, in the early days, users were dogged by slow connections, complex set-up regimes, expensive subscriptions and slow initial account creation. Now I can go to any web page, or dial a number using a set-up program on a free CD-ROM, and create myself a functioning Internet web and e-mail account within less than a minute. And all this will cost me nothing at all, and enhanced services will be available to me at a relatively low and affordable extra charge.

There are also many other changes which affect all of us but are not customer-driven, particularly in the service industry. In some cases, service industries have undertaken cost and overhead reduction measures that are not necessarily tailored to exactly what customers want but are, instead, for internal reasons. Automating telephone-based services is never popular, replacing bank clerks with machines and Internet services may suit some but causes difficulties for many others, and some shops have reduced their floor staff to such an extent that it is almost impossible to make a purchase unless one knows exactly what one wants. Nevertheless, this still represents change and development. Any organization offering comparable services must rise to the challenge and either follow the trend or find some way of building better customer service at an acceptable price. Either way, there is constant pressure to change. Nobody can afford to sit still and elect not to adapt to an ever-shifting environment.

THE PACE OF CHANGE

Many commerce watchers out there are waiting for the rate of growth and change to slow down: 'It can't go on like this forever,' they cry. This belief is based on two precepts: first, that people cannot sustain prolonged periods of energetic activity indefinitely – they need to rest occasionally; second, that industrial history is generally characterized by spurts of activity followed by periods of stabilization. Although this sounds entirely reasonable, what is actually happening does not seem to fit these ideas. In fact, what we are seeing is growth that begets further growth; each innovation fuels further ideas and activity in another direction, rather like some continuous, global brainstorming session.

The limiting factor on development and change today is not a lack of ideas or capability but a lack of willingness to deal with the influx of change. Consider the raging debates over genetic technology which really only began to warm up at the end of the twentieth century. The question of how much research and application of animal cloning, growth of replacement human tissue or commercial use of genetically modified plants is not about how easy or expensive it is but about whether we actually want it. At first sight it is difficult to imagine anybody buying pork which has been bred to contain a spinach gene, but it is available. The problem is that once the capability to do these things has been developed, it is hard to discard it, and resistance will probably only delay its introduction rather than prevent it. A new technology or approach will only be assigned to the waste bin if it proves to be useless or is superseded by something better. The nuclear generation of electricity is a case in point; it has its problems but is arguably cleaner if the plant can be made safe and the waste material can be adequately disposed of. Therefore it remains in use, despite the fact that some people do not like it. Eventually, it will decline in use, but only when a new development supersedes it in terms of cheapness or ease of production. There will always be useful new developments; if we do not like them, our only real chance of consigning them to the waste bin is to quickly develop something even better.

Since new ideas keep coming and we cannot stop them, we will have to accept that change is here to stay. Society will not need to rest and take stock because if some of the population become tired or burnt-out, there will always be someone with more energy and even newer ideas to take their place. What we need is the ability to gear our lives, culture and, in the context of this book, our business operations to cope with that constant change.

Here, however, lies the dilemma. If we really believe that change demands a constant injection of new blood and leaves a trail of casualties in its wake, then we are dooming the majority of people to be thrown on to the scrap heap at some point in their careers. Surely we cannot afford to do that? Demographics show that, as childhood mortality decreases and the length of time spent both in education and retirement increase, the proportion of the population actually working to provide wealth to support everybody will diminish. If that is so, we cannot compound the problem by allowing some of them to fall out of the system simply because they cannot cope with change.

Of course, the problem is not quite as bad as I may have painted it. It requires one level of energy to create an innovation and another to deal with it. Whilst it might be hard to see how any but an exceptional handful can remain at their peak of creativity all their working lives (which is why the few prolific and talented artists become household names and the rest fade into obscurity), it is reasonable to suppose that we can organize things to help everybody cope with the changes that are happening around them.

Since the pace of change is unlikely to decrease, and will probably even increase, we have to find ways of coping with the uncertainty that it brings and ensuring that everybody in the organization is coping with it too. After all, an organization, no matter how automated, is its people; if everybody left tomorrow there would be nothing for our computers and robots to do. And it is people that make change happen; machines are no good at coping with change at all – at least, not on their own.

The techniques for managing change are many, varied and, hopefully, changing too – developing to keep pace with what is going on in the business world. I deal with just one part of managing change in this book. Methods and ideas for determining how well people are coping with situations or developments: this aspect of change is often neglected; change agents are often keen to do the apparently correct thing and then hurry on to the next step, without making any rigorous effort to see what impact it has had on the organization's people. This book explores the ways in which we can measure what our people are doing and feeling to make us better able to deal with their approach and inputs to the organization as a whole.

THE APPEARANCE OF CHANGE

Of course, as soon as I state that everything is constantly changing, it is only natural to react by thinking of a number of examples where things have remained fairly constant for a while. Certainly these exist. Ever-faster change is a global truth but there are inevitably pockets of stability, some of them quite prolonged. This does not mean that the topic of this book is irrelevant; it is always important to know the state of the organization's people since their energy, commitment, motivation, loyalty and other attributes can all alter (usually in a negative direction) over time even in a static environment. The need is greater, though, when change is taking place since, frankly, managing people is more difficult during such circumstances. We need to know the impacts of what is happening so that we can make things move in the direction that we wish them to. And anyone who says that their organization never changes, and will never have any need to, had better remove their blindfold quickly before they find their livelihood disappearing into history along with the likes of slide rule manufacturers, the British volume motorcycle industry or traditional catalogue printers (whose work has dwindled as publishers decide to place their catalogues on the Internet).

KNOWING WHERE WE ARE

One of the best things that we can do to help us cope with fast and continuous change is to monitor ourselves so that we know where we are and how well we are doing. A business change is like a physical journey; we cannot decide the direction in which we should head, the route we should take nor how quickly we should travel unless we know our current position.

Organizations employ a variety of techniques to gain a picture of their current status, most of which end up in some sort of evaluation. This might be in the form of 'good', 'moderate', 'bad' and so on or could be slightly more scientific such as reporting an initiative as 30 per cent complete. What is needed is a rigorous approach that gives us an understanding of what the output means and enables us to compare it to outputs gained from previous evaluations so that we can see how far we have moved (backwards or forwards) since the previous assessment.

I have often been told, when suggesting a rigorous self-evaluation programme to a busy executive, that a time of change is not the best time to do it. After all, they say, they are busy trying to implement the change itself and do not need the distraction; moreover, it is hard to pin down a moving target. I believe that this is the complete opposite of the truth; the only reason that I hear such things is because the person already feels hard-pressed and is horrified at the thought of extra work. When we are changing we need to monitor exactly what we are doing so that we can ensure that the change does not damage us or take us to a position where we do not wish to be. Measuring our status when we are doing nothing new is unlikely to yield interesting information. Returning to the travel analogy, I need to constantly look at my speed, progress towards my destination and relative position to other vehicles when I am driving along the motorway, yet can afford to close my eyes and relax when I am parked. And, besides, if we only measure ourselves in times of stability, we will never get around to it, since, as I have argued, change is constant and increasing.

Mind you, we also need to monitor anything that is currently stable, because we need to be prepared for the inevitable external pressure that will require it to change or we will want to change it ourselves in order to maintain our innovative lead.

PROCESS AND PEOPLE MONITORING

Once the idea of monitoring themselves and obtaining a full picture of their position has been accepted, most organizations begin by measuring two things – customer satisfaction and the performance levels of their processes.

Customer satisfaction measurement is usually the prerogative of either the marketing or quality functions and involves a mixture of looking at existing process data as well as some direct and indirect input from actual customers and players in the supply chain. It requires careful interpretation to be meaningful and is often, therefore, outsourced to specialists, or at least treated as something separate from, and different to, other measurements.

Process performance measurement is about measuring the way in which we are successful in doing what our organization is set up to achieve. In *The Organizational Measurement Manual*, a companion to this book, I explained that process performance measurement is established by:

1. defining our key processes
2. identifying the customers for those processes
3. understanding overall customer requirements for each process and process output
4. turning those requirements into deliverable characteristics that we can quantify
5. setting target limits for those characteristics
6. regularly and constantly measuring the characteristics
7. comparing the results against targets and taking firm action where indicated.

This is reasonably easy to do, even though for some non-technical processes it may require a little more thought and planning than, for example, a production process that aims to produce a widget of a certain size. What is missing is some measurement of how our people are dealing with external and internal demands and expectations. This is probably not dealt with as frequently as the 'harder' topics because it is much more difficult to do. With a little effort, I can measure how long it takes a form to be fully processed through all departments but I will find it much harder to measure loyalty, trust or job satisfaction. Yet, if, as I have suggested, our people are the key to our success, then knowing how well they are doing is vital. We can design the best paperwork processes in the world but they are useless if the people managing it are demotivated and uninterested.

'Ah, but what about employee surveys?' you may ask. Certainly these are used as a way of measuring a number of factors related to the people working in an organization and can be effective if used well, although they do have their limitations. They are not, however, common. Employee surveys tend to be used in only the largest organizations and then only occasionally, or perhaps once a year. Great use can be made of surveys for understanding how people feel, or at least how they choose to say they feel. However, we need to understand how best to use them and what the results mean as well as appreciate the fact that a single survey conducted in a fit of enthusiasm has a limited value on its own. We will also discover, as this book proceeds, that a survey is not the only way of monitoring factors relating to the people in our organization.

CUSTOMER EXPECTATIONS

As I have mentioned, much of the constant push for change derives from customer expectations. Whether these expectations are themselves fuelled by what we and our competitors are doing is, to some extent, irrelevant; if the customer wants something then we have to strive to provide it, regardless of the cause of that desire.

Ever more demanding customers have an impact on our people. Customers expect the people in the supplier organization not only to operate good processes but also do so in a cheerful, friendly, positive and accessible way. Gone are the days when we were treated badly by front-line service staff (bank officials, doctor's receptionists and upmarket department store sales staff spring immediately to mind) and were grateful that they would deign to deal with us at all. Now customers want to be treated like royalty, but usually with a touch of friendliness thrown in. This can cause a degree of stress amongst our people who may not naturally be inclined to be friendly and helpful yet feel obliged to 'put on a face'. On the other hand, if such an approach is done well it can create a much greater enthusiasm amongst staff for really working with the customer for mutual benefit.

Thus, to satisfactorily deal with customer expectations we not only need to determine what customers want, measure the success of our processes at satisfying those desires and evaluate customer satisfaction, we also need to have ways of determining what impact customer demands are having on our people and how those people are dealing with them. Undertaking these tasks is not just about being a socially responsible employer or trying to purvey some New-Age image, it is about making the best use of the human resources at our disposal for the benefit of our organization, our customers and our employees together.

I ought to mention here that linking what our people do with the ideals of good customer service is not about the degradation of human dignity or encouraging obsequiousness. In terms of service, customers are looking for friendliness, speed, energy and ability. Fawning sycophancy is not welcome and is as likely to put customers off as arrogant indifference. I wrote this book while the BBC drama series *Monarch of the Glen*, set in a large ancestral home with a number of family servants, was playing. The character portrayed as the maid-cum-cook-cum-housekeeper was energetic, slightly brash, imaginative and mildly irreverent, yet she was immensely likeable and seemed to represent the ideal employee for the family (in fact, so ideal that her worth was ultimately recognized through her betrothal to the lead character). She seemed in no way demeaned by her status as a servant and gave the impression that she would never involve herself in any activity that was against her principles. I see the same even in everyday places such as supermarkets; I feel much better served by a cashier who cracks a joke and passes the time of day than by one who is stuffily polite.

This is exactly what we want to encourage amongst our own people. We want them to enjoy dealing with customers and make it a pleasurable experience from both sides. So, measuring how well our organization's employees are doing is not for the purpose of beating them into line but to see whether we are creating the right environment and allowing their energy and enjoyment to thrive. In fact, the whole approach that I describe in subsequent chapters is based on the assumption that employee measurement is about supporting our people, not blaming or criticizing them.

KNOWING OUR STRATEGIES AND OBJECTIVES

It is all very well saying that we must compete or that we need to keep ahead of our competitors or monitor how well we are doing, but how do we know how well we have done? We can define and measure numerical values that represent some assessment of customer satisfaction but we often then ask ourselves what that measure means or even whether it is enumerating the right thing.

To overcome this problem we need to know what our organization is all about. We have to ask ourselves what we want to achieve (in addition to making a profit or meeting our budget) and how. Then we will need to answer our own questions by examining why we do our jobs in the first place and deciding the way in which we wish our organization to be run. The outcome of all this will be a set of overall objectives and strategies.

Objectives are the things that we wish to achieve, such as financial targets, the type of internal culture we wish to have, which customers we want to concentrate on, new areas that we wish to penetrate and so on. Strategies are the broad approaches that we wish to use to achieve those objectives (following the military model, the detailed ways in which we progress towards our objectives are often referred to as tactics). Strategies can encompass recruitment policies, behavioural norms, systems development approaches and organizational design. These are not ends in their own right but are there to achieve the stated objectives.

If we know where we want to be and the means by which we intend to get there, it is much easier to decide what we want to measure. For example, there may be little value in measuring the technical parameter of product reliability if we wish to achieve our objective of gaining high market share through rapid product churn. Or, from a people perspective, there is no point in evaluating long-term career progression planning if our strategy is to employ short-term casual labour.

MISSION STATEMENTS

The highest-level objectives are often put forward in the form of a mission statement – a paragraph or so of carefully chosen words that set out the overall idea of where the company wishes to be. Mission statements fluctuate in popularity. At one time business advisers would have drawn a sharp disapproving intake of breath if confronted with a client who did not have a defined and publicized mission statement, but nowadays people tend to view it as something that can be employed where appropriate and as just another option that a company may choose.

Although mission statements are a common way of defining the overall objectives, I have some problems with them. Although many of them may have brought the benefit of bringing senior managers together to talk about what they want to achieve, as a means of driving the organization they often lack something. My first problem is that they are almost always too vague or wordy to be meaningful. They often say something like:

> 'It is our mission to be recognized as the world's leading supplier of cooking aids in the domestic market.'

Whilst statements such as this aim to specify the market in which the company operates (although often the issue is fudged to allow for possible future product or service developments), what they actually want to do is less clear. What does 'the leading supplier' mean? It could suggest:

- that the company will sell more than any other single competitor
- that market growth will be faster than for any other competitor
- that the products will have more features than those of any competitor
- that the company will make more profit each year than any other competitor
- that the company's brand will be better known than anybody else's
- that the company will have a bigger market capitalization than any other competitor
- that market surveys will show that customers are better satisfied than those of the competitors.

Each of these definitions is very different and would require different strategies to attain. We could also then debate some of the other details in the statement such as 'supplier': does this mean that we will sell products that we ourselves design and make, or will we just be a sales organization selling other people's products?

My second problem relates to the creation of the closely worded statement itself. Experience shows that mission statements defined around a carefully chosen set of words tend to emphasize the precise nature of the words and not the message behind them. Employees are encouraged to be able to quote the statement verbatim and any related presentation by managers uses a repetition of the exact phrase. This hinders belief in the principles involved. Having faith does not require the ability to quote from Scripture (in fact, in Christian mythology the Devil can quote scripture better than anybody else). It is better to have people who understand and believe in the ideas behind our overall purpose; the best companies have people who are keen to tell visitors about 'the way things are done here' whereas weak cultures are characterized by groans whenever the topic of vision and direction is mentioned.

There is nothing wrong with reaching agreements about where you wish the organization to go and how it should get there. It is best, though, to concentrate on living and discussing the agreed approach so that it becomes inbred, rather than issue a set of trite words and rely on their memorization to create the right culture.

DEALING WITH UNCERTAINTY

One of the things created by rapid and constant change is uncertainty. Although we can safely say that we will continue to see change in all areas of our working lives, it is impossible to predict with perfect accuracy what form that change will take. I believe that the need to protect the environment, for example, will have a profound impact on how we choose products and services and will reverse some aspects of the globalization trend. Other writers have written extensively on how the Internet and the communications revolution will affect the future. Yet others have made predictions about the effects of genetic engineering, bacterial resistance to antibiotics, the growth of Islam against a background of decline in most other world religions, or new innovations in space exploration. Many of these may prove true but it is unlikely that any futurist has the future completely sewn up. In any case, the world is a complex system and every change has a relation to others so that the future shape of the business community could take a myriad forms, dependent on thousands of contributory factors.

Even less certain are the working patterns and associated requirements for individual workers. Even if we could predict the forward direction of technological and sociological change it would still be almost impossible to see how that would affect the working lives of our existing employees. Organizations react not only to the external environment but also to their perceived position within it, which in turn is a result of developments and initiatives, so that, in all likelihood, the form of our company will be very different in ten years' time. As the shape of external influences themselves are uncertain, it is impossible to predict what is in store for any one of us.

Measurement, then, is becoming increasingly important. If we measure our performance and make those measurements available to all our people, then they have a better chance of understanding what is going on and seeing how things are changing. If we can also measure how the reactions, abilities and feelings of those people are altering, then we can quickly see where a change is likely to lead to personnel problems and take actions to put ourselves back on course. Early, unrestricted business process re-engineering initiatives were largely seen to be badly flawed because they not only failed to consider in advance how people would deal with the changes but also made no attempt to examine their reactions afterwards; low morale and falling performance only revealed themselves when they showed up in other areas, by which time the damage was very costly to repair.

The need to measure is just as important when the future is uncertain as when we have a clear picture of our forward development. If our people cannot cope with the associated uncertainty then our entire organization will not be able to manage the necessary changes and we will hit the crash barriers while our competitors go on to take the championship cup.

OPERATIONAL VERSUS STRATEGIC MEASUREMENT

When we decide that we wish to measure something we also have to decide who will use the results and to what purpose. A key question is whether the measurement is a broad look at what the organization is doing and how it is performing or whether we are examining one particular aspect of performance or even looking closely at a characteristic of an individual process. In *The Organizational Measurement Manual*, this was illustrated by a 'measurement continuum', as shown in Figure 1.1.

A measurement that constitutes a look at the whole picture, the type typically desired by board members and senior managers who wish to have all-encompassing metrics that describe such things as profit, sales volume, market share, growth, share value and customer satisfaction ratings. These are affected by a large number of different activities that occur in the organization, and success or failure can rarely be directly attributed to just one factor. Profit, for example, is probably affected by almost

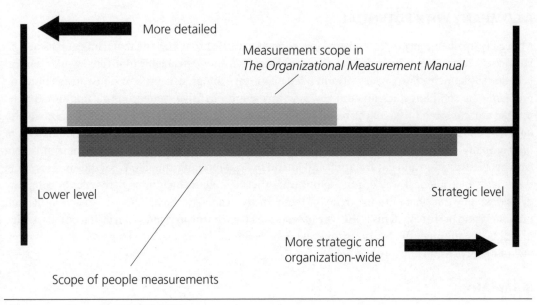

Figure 1.1   The measurement continuum

every activity, to a greater or lesser extent. Some activities may have an indirect impact on profit, and many others will create small or delayed impacts, but everybody contributes. Such measurements belong at the far right of the continuum. They are highly strategic and are used to decide whether the organization as a whole is doing as well as would be liked.

At the other end of the continuum, on the far left, there are measurements that are of use to the team that directly controls a process or function. These would look at specific characteristics of the process that are directly within the control of the team and relate to characteristics which directly or indirectly relate to requirements of process customers. Such measurements will be used to make immediate adjustments or improvements to the process being monitored. They are of little interest to senior managers; indeed, it is a bad idea to encourage those at the most strategic level of the organization to pay attention to detailed process metrics since they may misinterpret minor variations and use them as a reason to start witch-hunts.

Measurements of people-based issues can also fit well into the model shown in Figure 1.1. There are some overall attributes that can be measured at the corporate, strategic level. These simply look at the overall ratings of any of the personal feelings or attitudes that we wish to measure and tell us how well we are doing on the whole and whether our actions seem to be making the whole workforce feel better or worse, or whether we are maintaining the status quo. Measurements towards the left side of the continuum may well be similar in name but would typically look at a smaller population – for example, the rating for a single work team.

Thus there is a slightly different approach for people-based issues. Technical and functional measurements often differ markedly between process and strategic levels (for example, profit versus spindle diameter) whereas people-based issues may be identical at both levels but applied to a different number and variety of people.

When we aim to design people measurements we need to bear Figure 1.1 in mind. For a fully effective approach we will have to monitor our people at several points along the continuum. This is discussed in more detail in Chapter Four.

A COMPANY WITH POTENTIAL

A typically small, but successful and growing, company will be broadly aware that it relies on its people for success. Its managers have the overall aim of having an energetic, highly motivated workforce and occasionally launch a flurry of activity intended to improve things, usually in response to an emerging problem. The company does not, though, have any comprehensive strategy for making sure that its people are contented and effective, nor does it have any scientific or controlled approach to understanding any of the issues related to its employees. Nevertheless, the directors and managers of the company do have a vague feeling that they should be doing more to monitor and promote employee satisfaction and contribution and intend to do something about it. What they need is some systematic and practical way of finding out what their people feel and how they react to company decisions, now that there are too many of them for the leaders to be able to know each individual intimately and personally. This is the type of scenario I have borne in mind when laying out the advice in this book, although the lessons should be equally applicable to any size or type of organization, including service and non-profit groups.

SUMMARY

- Every programme and initiative that is intended to make us more effective and competitive must rely on people to make it happen.
- We all need to compete – even where our organization is seen as a public service or is not-for-profit.
- The pace of change in modern society is rapid and we need to equip our people to keep abreast of it.
- With change happening so rapidly, it is important to know where we are so that we can see where we should be going.
- Measuring performance helps us know where we are.
- Since people are key to the future of our business, it is just as important to measure people as it is to measure the principal business processes.
- Understanding our forward path by setting objectives and strategies helps us better deal with change and make the best use of our measurements.
- Knowing what our forward strategy means is more important than memorizing a mission or policy statement.
- Measurements can be strategic, taking a broad view with multiple inputs, or can relate to specific characteristics of individual processes; both are applicable to the measurement of people.

CHAPTER TWO

Understanding People

THE IMPORTANCE OF PEOPLE

It is impossible to be too devoted to ensuring that we are making the best use of our people. Highly motivated people who are performing at their peak will make a far greater contribution to success than will any organizational structure, information system or management tool that is sold as a solution to a company's needs. This is not to say that such things have no value, it is just that they can only produce their greatest benefits if we are managing our people well. In fact, many of them will produce no benefits at all if we do not have our people tuned to the intended objectives; investment in sophisticated sales tracking and planning software is a waste if our salespeople have no energy and enthusiasm for approaching potential new customers.

This does not mean that we should be managing people so that they totally conform to some predefined image of the ideal worker. Wanting everybody to support corporate objectives and appear happy in doing so does involve creating an Orwellian Thought Police to monitor them, or somehow establishing a Brave New World where workers at different levels are manipulated to be happy with their lot. On the other hand, if we just let people get on with their jobs and pay no attention to whether or not they are contented or to what effect our activities are having on their morale, they are soon likely to drift away from the desired corporate direction. Just as important, if we do not have some way of evaluating the personnel effects of what we are doing, we may blithely believe that we are encouraging high performance when in fact we are not. As mentioned in Chapter One, this is even more true in a time of change, when people's feelings and attitudes are bound to alter, yet, without measuring, we have little real knowledge of the way in which that alteration is being manifested.

WHAT WE ARE LOOKING FOR

Exactly what we should be seeking in the people with whom we work is a matter for corporate preferences and circumstances. My own preferences would be to seek among the workforce the sort of dynamic, enthusiastic, flexible and innovative approaches that characterize the most exciting of today's organizations. You, as a reader, however, may have other priorities. I remember once having a long debate with a group of line managers from a high-volume factory in which they argued most strongly that many of the production floor workers had no interest in doing anything other than the minimum needed to get paid and not be sacked. Although I put the case for increasing their interest by allowing the operators greater freedom, their point of view, and the examples that they gave to support it, seemed to have some validity in their particular situation.

Your own circumstances may dictate specific, individual requirements. For example, you may wish to have a workforce that is very good at doing what it is told (a misunderstood, but still vital, requirement in the military establishment). Alternatively, the ability to convey a particular disposition may be important, such as for theme park entertainers or, at the other end of the spectrum, employees of funeral directors.

The range of what we could measure and what is correct to measure is as wide as the different types of commercial and public service company that exist in all modern economies. Because of this, it is not my intention here to list the particular people characteristics that you should be measuring and what the desired result should be, but to draw your attention to the sorts of thing that you could measure, which may not be monitored in conventional management programmes. Most organizations have measurements of one form or another, but the majority of these are system-based, or possibly look at process performance, and are not aimed directly at people. If people are the one feature of an enterprise that most affect its success, then surely it follows that measuring them is just as important as measuring the other contributory factors.

This does not mean that other measurements are irrelevant when thinking about evaluating our people. Analysis of how well processes operate can be a key indicator of how well people are functioning, especially when viewed over time; a decrease in performance when the system and environmental aspects of a process remain constant could be an indication of falling motivation, for example. In many cases, though, if you are trying to measure personal issues, it is better to do this directly, than try to guess them from other data that may be an indirect people indicator. Just as we do not measure vehicle height from the road to gauge our tyre pressure, so we should not measure response times to find out how enthusiastic our telephone staff are.

This is a very important point. Many managers will argue that, since they are seeking profit, sales volume, output and so on, only that information is valuable; everything else just contributes to the primary goal. In one sense this is true, but organizations are complex and it may not be immediately obvious why a key metric is falling. If we measure the subsidiary factors that have an impact on our desired goals, then we are more likely to pinpoint the cause of a change and take the appropriate action. Using the vehicle example again, what we are looking for is a comfortable and safe ride, but one of the things that we actually measure is the tyre pressure since it directly contributes to that objective.

> **TIP**
> Watch how measurements are used in your organization; if a poor set of data results in somebody senior stalking around in a bad mood and making random decisions, perhaps the right level of detail is not being measured.

'IT'S NOT PERSONAL'

When we talk of evaluating people, many readers will inevitably interpret this as methods of conducting personal performance appraisal. While it is certainly possible that some of the ideas mentioned here could be used to assess individuals, there is also little clear distinction between methods that are aimed at groups and large populations and those that target individuals. To my mind, however, there is one special difference between management techniques for giving personal feedback and counselling and those aimed at team or organizational management – namely, that the actions resulting from a personal appraisal interview are usually seen as being the responsibility of the person being appraised, whereas actions from the general measurement of people-based issues lies with those managing the activities. Thus if we find that most of our people are dissatisfied, slow, fearful, disloyal and so on, then the responsibility lies with those leading the organization to manage things better to correct those faults. This is different to the situation where an individual in an otherwise loyal environment is found to be acting against the company's interests and needs to correct their own behaviour.

A guiding principle for many of these measurements, then, is 'it's not personal'. If we are monitoring how people feel and behave, we have to understand that its purpose should be to consider the overall position and the effect that our actions are having, not to give us an opportunity to pick on an individual for minor perceived flaws. Even if our results were to be based on an extreme sampling technique which considers the views and feelings of just one person, they should be judged as an indicator of the whole. Personal evaluation should be left to the performance appraisal process.

TAKING ACCOUNT OF PEOPLE

Many of us who have been involved in changing the way that organizations work, or in measuring how well (or badly) they operate, have been brought up on process thinking. This approach leads us to look at work processes, create a system boundary around them and then look at how the system could be operated more efficiently or effectively. However. such techniques rarely try to model the influence of personal interactions on the overall process. They may look at how well an individual performs as part of the system, but the accompanying human emotions and conditions can easily be overlooked. What is needed is a systems approach that looks not only at the technical process with its associated inputs and outputs but also looks at the personal inputs, processes and outputs of those employed within the system. I discuss this in more detail under 'Aspects of Human Contribution' below.

LEVELS OF PERSONAL REACTION

If we use an approach that does take account of people, we need to do it on three levels.

The *first level* is to be able to judge the ways in which our activities are likely to impact on the people that carry them out or are affected by them. This requires us to look at the system, what it is intended to perform and the main inputs and outputs. From this we should be able to see how people interact with the system. Information inputs and outputs will require communication with other systems and processes which can be a source of motivation or stress; materials and product movements can cause physical tiredness and may represent health safety hazards or, where people themselves are part of an input or output (such as in many human resources processes), carrying out the process could mean that they have to cope with changes and disruption. Similarly the processes themselves can have an influence, such as those which require extensive personal travel, extended working hours, long periods of solitude or the ability to quickly adapt to new situations.

The *second level* is the understanding of exactly how much each aspect does affect the people in the system. This is where measurement comes in, using structured techniques to provide some form of quantitative or similar analysis to give a detailed picture of both the average level of response to a system or situation and the spread of reactions. For example, it is all very well to know that the average level of fatigue is reasonably low, but if this average is composed of responses from one group that is full of energy together with another that is completely drained, then we clearly need to take action despite the generally positive overall result. The overall measurement is important because it tells us the broad effect of our activities; the spread may help us discover whether different groups or teams feel differently and how much of a gap there is between the 'best' and the 'worst' of our people.

For those familiar with the ideas of statistical process control, this double approach to measurement is similar to the $\bar{X}$ and $\bar{R}$ approach where both sample means and ranges are plotted. Although this book deals with measurement of personal factors rather than operational ones, I give a conventional explanation of the mean and range approaches here, so that we have a sufficient foundation for using the concept as the book progresses.

To see how the technique works, it is best to work on a sample of data. In Table 2.1, I have shown the sizes of a sample of products taken from a storeroom. The mean (average) size is calculated by summing all the individual sizes and dividing by the number in the sample (10). This gives an average product size of 20.53 mm. If asked, for example, how big the products are, we could answer that they are about 20.5 mm, but that each one may vary from that size slightly. To give the full picture we also need to find the range, which is calculated by taking the smallest size (20 mm) from the largest (21.1 mm) giving a range of 1.1 mm. That is, the size of the product varies as much as 1.1 mm in the sample chosen. At the simplest level of treatment, we simply then plot the mean and the range on a line graph and then add further points as we measure further samples. This is done by using the latest few measurements as the data set. For example, as we have calculated our mean and range using the ten measurements shown in Table 2.1, it would be a good starting point to use ten as our data set. Consequently, our next mean would be calculated by adding the results from items 2 to 11, then dividing by ten, the following mean would use measurements 3 to 12, and so on. This process tells us how the overall situation is moving, and we would probably use a graph on which we would plot each successive mean and range to give us a visual picture of the trends. The actual number of points used for each calculation depends on the type of measurement and personal preference. For the moving mean you can use as few as three points but remember that the smaller the data set used, the less meaningful the range calculation is. If we consider the extreme of only using two points, the range will be highly variable; on the other hand, too many points will result in a graph that hardly moves.

Table 2.1   Samples for mean and range calculations

Sample number	Size (mm)
1	20.4
2	20.0
3	21.1
4	20.5
5	20.4
6	20.8
7	20.1
8	20.8
9	20.9
10	20.3

From these graphs we can tell whether the average level is rising or falling and whether the process is becoming more variable. For example, if the range is increasing with time, our control over the product size is becoming looser and our average value is becoming less meaningful.

More complex extensions of this idea allow for the use of the mean values from a number of samples or statistical analyses which give a picture of the shape, not just the overall magnitude, of the range. However, since the measurement of people is more about how to quantify the situation in the first place, rather than how to analyse raw data, some of these more advanced techniques are not applicable to our discussion here. Nevertheless, it is worth considering the use of a measurement of spread such as standard deviation to describe how widely the measurements vary. Range is a simple, easily understandable factor to calculate but it has some disadvantages, the main one being that in a population of any size, where the possible values are fixed (for example, 1 to 10 on a questionnaire) then it is fairly obvious that we will quickly get to the point where we can guarantee that every measurement will show a range of 9, because there will always be at least one person at each extreme. To obtain a better picture of how broadly spread the measurements are, a more sophisticated sum is needed. I will not try to define standard deviation in this chapter, but it is worth knowing that it is akin to range, but also shows whether the variation is caused by just a few people deviating from a central point or whether we have a very broad spread. This is done by calculating a standard deviation from a set of numbers; the bigger the standard deviation the more the spread.

> TIP
>
> Most of us do not need to know specifically how standard deviation is calculated, only that it indicates spread, so it is easiest just to type all our numbers into a spreadsheet and let the computer tell us what the standard deviation is.

If the distribution of data that we gain from our measurements is normal, 68 per cent of all observations will fall within +1 or −1 standard deviation from the mean value, 95 per cent will fall within two standard deviations and 99.7 per cent will fall within three standard deviations. There are also definitions for the percentages at further spreads from the mean, but the numbers then become extremely close to 100 per cent. For our purposes we can consider that just about everything falls within three standard deviations of the mean. However, having given this information as background, we do not even really need to remember these figures; all that we need to know is that standard deviation measures spread, so that one measurement with a much higher standard deviation than another will mean that its data show wider opinions, behaviours and so on.

At the *third level* we must be committed to taking action on the results of our measurements. I have always made it my policy never to promise anything to a person at work that I am not sure that I can deliver. This has always been especially important for personal issues; there is little more demoralizing than promising a promotion, job move, pay rise or similar and then not delivering on that promise. The same applies to any measurement and evaluation programme; if we manage to convince people that it is worthwhile, there is nothing sinister about it and it is not personal, then all that effort will have been wasted if we do nothing with the results of our analyses. We will have wasted our own time and will have caused disillusionment amongst the people that we are measuring. As part of our planning of the measurement programme, we will have to identify times and people to look at the data produced and run correction or improvement projects in the appropriate areas.

I cannot overemphasize the importance of this need to take visible action. I spent a good deal of time working with a large company that had adopted a highly structured TQM (total quality management) programme designed by a reputable team of consultants from the USA. However, the leaders of the company had little intention of actually changing anything; rather, they wanted the seminars, training and team meetings to take place so that they could inform the parent company that they were 'a TQM organization'. This was not only a waste of time but was actually damaging as employees' motivation and commitment plummeted once they realized the true situation. It is difficult to motivate a cynical workforce to any subsequent 'real' initiatives that the organization wishes to adopt. This type of situation must clearly be avoided by anyone wishing to take a serious look at the way in which their people contribute to the organization. Those with decision-making ability have to be quite clear that they are prepared to make changes and spend the time and money to do so, while also understanding that some of the things that they may be required to do could be uncomfortable for them.

ASPECTS OF HUMAN CONTRIBUTION

In Chapter Four we will deal with the specifics of what we might actually measure. Before we do that, though, it is worth looking at the overall way in which people can contribute to the success of an enterprise. As a basic foundation, they need the capability to make things work well and the will and the power to do so. Then, when they have actually achieved something worthwhile, they need to sustain the benefits of their work.

I would like to think of elements of success in general business terms, so I have classified them as: foundation, fuel, results and support. I will explain below what I mean by each of these.

FOUNDATION

The foundation element provides people's fundamental ability to carry out their work. It is the human equivalent of the design throughput rate of a machine, the speed of a microprocessor or the load-bearing capacity of a crane. Much of the measurement in this case will be concerned with looking at concrete factors that rarely or slowly change, such as experience levels and qualifications.

This factor is strongly influenced by the conditions of employment controlled by management. These include:

- contracted working hours (setting the amount of time that a person is available to work)
- recruitment policy (setting the calibre of person that we employ, including such things as qualification, experience and skill levels)
- remuneration policy (related to recruitment policy, having a direct impact on the attraction and retention of the most skilled employees)
- company culture (possibly determining how fast and flexibly people work, how closely they follow procedures and the overall amount of effort that is 'normal' in the organization).

Working hours, for example, directly relate to an employee's capacity since a full-time worker present for 36 hours per week will have, nominally, double the capacity of a part-time person working 18 hours per week. We must, however, ensure that we know what we are measuring when looking at this or any of the other categories. For instance, capacity related to working hours is not linear; there is some time lost at the start and finish of each day in exchanging pleasantries with colleagues, hanging up the coat, logging on to the network and obtaining the first cup of coffee. We should also bear in mind that if we increase the hours too far, we begin to see only marginal increases in capacity since tiredness, stress and boredom (not necessarily all together) can set in.

FUEL

Once we have sufficient innate capacity to be able to fulfil our business processes, the amount, type and frequency of 'fuel' will determine how fast and far we can go. Fuel represents the way in which an organization encourages its people to perform better. Activities under this category could include:

- continuing training and other forms of personal development
- personal encouragement and 'positive strokes' (a popular American term for 'praise')
- a corporate culture that welcomes input from individuals
- an environment that encourages excellence.

Some of these fuelling elements are rather difficult to measure and define quantitatively. This should not deter us, however, since the whole subject of employee measurement needs applied effort to grasp; we simply need to employ some imagination and persistence.

The cultural and environmental constituents of fuel are probably the most important. The roses of success need a fertile soil in which to grow; they are easily damaged by the presence of the wrong fundamental elements. Trust is a good example. I have encountered several organizations which trust their people's discretion so little that withdrawal of every small component or even stationery item from the stores is as painful as drawing teeth. Enthusiasm, speed, innovation and creativity can hardly flourish in such circumstances; indeed, people are likely to be inclined to do less since they know that their employer has little faith in them. Similarly, even in today's highly aware society, there are still organizations in which sexual harassment is so prevalent that the work of female employees is hampered by the need to avoid any situation which could be remotely threatening or damaging to their reputation. Conversely, a strong culture in which desirable values are publicly rewarded and undesirable behaviours are just as publicly vilified gives every employee the freedom to utilize a far greater proportion of their potential.

Fuel can also be represented by qualities that the people themselves put into their work, such as personal enthusiasm. Measuring these is more about looking at how the individual behaves than how the organization contributes to success through people.

RESULTS

Results is the area of personal performance that is most familiar to managers. Business leaders quickly grow to understand that they are often judged on immediate output metrics. The whole management by objectives (MBO) concept grew from output performance measurement, although it is now less fashionable, being seen as too narrowly focused and difficult to orient towards a broader business picture.

Yet, this is not to say that output measurements are not important. If it is the commercial manager's job to make sure that all customer order paperwork is dealt with on time, then the actual ratio of rapid to slow order processing is definitely of interest. We can consider this as a valid measurement as long as we do not see this as the only factor in determining how well the commercial manager has performed.

The types of results measurement that can be applied relate specifically to the individual job and are therefore too numerous to sensibly list here. They do, however, almost always fall into one of three categories:

- *quality* – whether the product or service has been delivered correctly and to the customer's satisfaction
- *delivery* – whether the product or service has been delivered on time
- *cost* – whether the product or service has been supplied within the allowed costs and budgetary constraints.

This is easily applied to a physical task such as asking somebody to build, say, a wooden cupboard. We want the finished article to be the right size, shape and appearance and wish it to be sturdy enough to do its intended job. We also want it when promised, not several weeks later, and we wish it to be reasonably priced.

We can also apply these categories to services or daily tasks. If I am repairing a domestic washing machine it needs to be restored to a state as close to its new condition as possible, the technician should arrive at my house at the promised time (a perennial complaint of many householders is that they wait at home all day for a tradesman who never turns up) and the cost should not be so prohibitive that I would not have been better off just throwing my old machine away and buying a new one.

As I have already mentioned, we must be careful about using the results category to measure people, despite the fact that results are the means by which many others will measure us. Very often, the results of an individual's activities are affected just as much by external factors as by their own performance. Indeed, well-accepted quality management doctrines argue that the majority of failures are caused by the corporate management and systems, not by the worker. It is possible to design measurement schemes that take account of this to some extent, as I have explored in *The Organizational Measurement Manual*, but we must beware of misinterpreting the results. An even bigger danger is often the tendency to concentrate on achieving the results that are being measured at the expense of those that are not being monitored, or less tangible factors. A simple example might be a call centre employee who is measured by the number of calls that they handle in a day, which may well lead them to terminate calls from customers before the caller feels that their problem has been fully addressed.

SUPPORT

Support is more than the equivalent of motor vehicle maintenance. It is about how well the organization seeks to aid its initiatives and supplement the work done by its people through continual understanding, correction and improvement.

Again, exactly how this aspect of the use of people manifests itself depends on the nature of the work involved. Typically, though, it can involve:

- the extent to which blame and criticism is attached to an error or whether undesirable episodes are treated as learning opportunities and areas for management improvement
- encouragement and the continued supply of resources to a project even when things are not going to plan or are going a little badly
- planning, to ensure that needs are predicted in a timely manner
- emergency preparedness, so that problems are handled in a professional manner without panic
- adoption of the Plan-Do-Check-Act approach
- availability and use of independent counsellors (that is, people with recognized authority and status who are not seen as the individual's boss).

As before, much of this is about the working environment. It represents the ability and willingness of the organization to help its people when there are projects, problems or changes to overcome.

Again, there are support aspects that are more within the control of the individual than of the organization. These might include the existence and strength of the person's own support network, such as family, professional institutions, social outlets and so on, that provide a way of helping them deal with stress, or their own approach to dealing with difficulties.

PERSONAL AND ORGANIZATIONAL INPUT

One thing that may have become apparent from the above is that there is another way of categorizing the human relations elements that we may wish to measure: personal and organizational. There are some work features and behavioural traits that we may wish to monitor that arise directly from how the individual or group feels and acts. There are others that represent aspects of the organization and how it is structured and run, that will in turn determine the way that people behave and react to situations.

These are not independent. The way in which the organization is set up will have a strong impact on the way in which people feel and act. In fact, it is sometimes argued that it will completely determine their response to certain stimuli, although this is probably too simple a view, since people always retain their individuality and the mind-set of their upbringing and personal lives, no matter how strong the company culture. There is also a reverse (albeit admittedly weaker) cause-and-effect relationship since organizations often set themselves up to allow for local and cultural factors, perhaps by providing multilingual signs, documentation and managers if they employ workers of varying national and ethnic origins.

We can use these interdependencies to measure both personal and organizational factors that relate to our specific area of interest. This will enable us to define the way in which the management of our people is arranged to work around, or make best use of, the way in which our people perform.

DETERMINING KEY SUCCESS FACTORS

Once we understand the types of issue that might affect the performance of our people, it is important to identify the key success factors (KSFs). Key success factors have long been used in many business and organizational initiatives to determine what is important and target effort towards those things. They are those few things that make the difference between success and failure and can make an enterprise succeed over its competitors. They often relate to an organization's performance in the marketplace. I have even seen a major telecommunications company that tried to design its entire organizational structure around its KSFs (although they called them *critical* success factors).

To illustrate the concept, let us look at an entrepreneurial team wishing to start a management training company. If they take it seriously and do some planning before launch, they may well try to identify their KSFs before they begin selling and running the training courses. Their first consideration is, typically, money. A training company, like any other, needs some early set-up funds but does not require large sums of capital for investment in plant; most of its costs are operational rather than depreciation. If we assume, then, that the owners have put enough into the venture to tide them over the initial business development period, then having sources of external finance is not a key factor. Since it is accepted in such businesses that most customers pay in advance yet most costs (hotels, subcontract staff, printing) are on credit terms, payment cash flow should not be a major issue either. Pricing is, however, critical since it must be high enough to project the right image and to ensure that the business is profitable, without being so high that it fails to attract all but the most cost-insensitive business.

Knowing what is the right thing to do in many situations is not a problem since good practice in industry is fairly well understood. This means that the 'technical' content of the training courses is not important. How well participants report on a course, however, often depends on how much they have enjoyed the experience. This means that the course designs and 'feel' have to be lively and participative, with plenty of games, humour and action.

Picking the right trainers is relatively important, but since there is a glut of freelance and employed trainers, good staff are not hard to find. Getting the courses filled, and convincing organizations to run extensive in-house programmes, on the other hand, is a difficult task and one that many training firms struggle with. So a strong sales culture is vital.

Discussions like this can reveal the few factors on which we must concentrate to really make certain that we succeed. In this case we have identified:

- pricing
- the fun element
- sales.

In sum, once we know what our key success factors are, we can then direct our efforts, and our associated measurements, most closely towards supporting them in order to achieve success.

PEOPLE SUCCESS FACTORS

It is not uncommon for organizations to attempt to define their business factors for success. In the training company example above, we looked at those things which make for overall market success. If, however, we wish to particularly consider the elements of the business that rely on people (and on which people rely) then we must think about the people success factors. These are the key factors that will lead to maximum personal satisfaction and the best use of our human resources.

People success factors could include any of the elements that we have discussed so far, and probably several others, as being worthy of measurement and consideration. What is important, though, is to judge which factors are key for our own business. Just as managing credit may be a key success factor for a manufacturing company but not for a management training provider, so there will be things that are vital to the success of one enterprise that are less important in another. The crucial task is to choose the right ones for our own circumstances. For example, it may be essential for some types of organization to recruit employees with specific qualifications, especially where those qualifications are a prerequisite to practising their trade or profession, such as in hospitals, law firms and road transport companies. On the other hand, organizations such as manufacturing or software companies will only look for qualifications as an indicator of knowledge, skill and experience and could well prefer evidence of flair and innovation over formal certification. In other cases, such as fast food outlets, a display of energy is important, whereas, for other professions – for instance, writers or accountants – a calm, studied approach may be more appropriate.

IDENTIFYING PRIMARY CONCERNS

Building on the understanding of the categories of human measurement and the key success factors for our business, it is important to understand our current main concerns. These are the things that are currently worrying us or where our efforts are being targeted and are seen as being the hottest topics of the moment for our organization. For instance, using the training company example, if we suddenly found that our largest competitor had just announced a service enabling its customers to obtain much of their training via an integrated web-based solution, it may be vital for us to either develop our own Internet product or position ourselves in such a way as to reduce the threat that it poses.

It is then possible to look at the people side of our concerns. So, for example, we may be faced with a global skills shortage, or poor availability of people with a wide linguistic capability, or a deteriorating professional image due to some media event.

At this point, readers may wonder about the difference between key success factors and primary concerns. After all, both represent the most significant things that we have to address in order to be successful. Their difference lies in their immediacy. Key success factors are intrinsic to our organization; if something is essential for our success today then it will continue to be so tomorrow. On the other hand, our most urgent concern could be temporary and will no longer be of interest to us once the crisis has passed. A good example of this was the so-called millennium bug – the fear that many computers would fail during the transition from 1999 to 2000 because a large number of older systems were programmed to only take account of the last two digits of the date. As soon as the feared date had passed, the effects of the Y2K problem (as it was known) were no longer of concern to anyone (except the occasional journalist and pundit who wanted to pick over its bones). There was no way in which fixing the millennium bug was an intrinsic success factor for businesses, yet it was a concern that, temporarily, dominated their workload. This is not to say that key success factors will never change, but their adaptation has a long timescale, typically taking place over years as the organization gradually evolves.

Thus we are likely to have a dual set of priorities: the underlying and long-term key success factors, sitting alongside the short-term primary concerns. A word of warning here: take care that primary concerns do not encourage you to deal only with today's issues because they are immediate and ignore the key success factors because their impact will not be felt until later. I have always kept in mind a diagram that I was shown in an early training course, reproduced here in Figure 2.1.

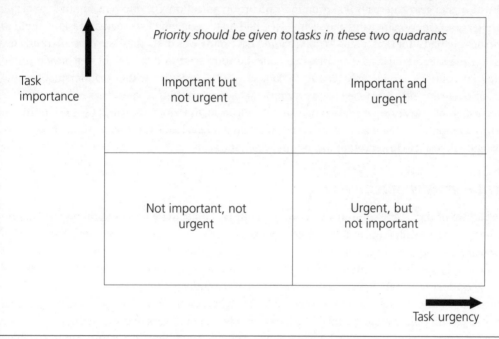

Figure 2.1   Task importance and urgency

The logic here is that we can assign strengths to any issue that we are now facing in two dimensions: urgency and importance. In this way, problems can range from not urgent and unimportant in the bottom left quadrant to urgent and important in the top right quadrant. We are all tempted to tackle tasks based on their urgency, not on their importance. Thus urgent, but unimportant, issues are dealt with before the important ones, when in fact it is probably better to tackle the important but not urgent topics and only deal with the trivial items if and when there is time. This needs to be borne in mind in our measurement programme; remember that just because an issue seems to warrant attention right now does not necessarily mean that it should be given priority over something much more important that is less urgent.

PINNING IT DOWN

So far, we have discussed categorizing the people-based elements in which we are interested and identifying our business's key success factors and its current main concerns. In each of these I have tried to give examples to illustrate the types of thing that we are looking for. In my own work, though, I have always found that just having an idea of the sort of thing I am interested in is not enough. Before I can really get to grips with a topic I need to refine that idea to understand exactly what it is that I am thinking about. Even then, once I think I understand exactly what I am looking at, as soon as I start to give it serious consideration a whole raft of questions creep out of the woodwork, all of which also need answering before I can actually tackle the issue.

It is essential to have the answers to all these questions in order to firmly pin down what we are seeking and to appreciate the details of what we are considering. I remember that, as a young manager in a Swiss electronics company, I had a general feeling that my team was not achieving as much as it could; my response was to explain, during the next team briefing session, that we were now going to move into a higher gear and really make our mark on the organization. Of course, my motivational talk had no effect whatsoever since the people involved had no idea of what I was actually asking them to do – and neither had I, for that matter! What I should have done was to spend some time analysing my impression and identifying some specifics that could be addressed, and this might well have resulted in increased overall effectiveness. Trying to look at the big picture without understanding the underlying detail is of little use when we are trying to achieve something as specific as measurement.

Once you think you know what areas need to be addressed, therefore, keep drilling down until you hit the firm foundation of your area of interest. Be certain that you know what issue you wish to tackle; being vague will result in low levels of success, or even none at all.

INTUITION VERSUS OBJECTIVITY

The whole aim of this book is to introduce some rigour and objectivity into determining the nature and strength of issues affecting and controlled by people. As such, I have stressed the importance of being systematic and objective. This involves understanding exactly what we wish to evaluate, how it relates to the things that are important for the business, making judgements on a firm basis and having a good decision-making system for dealing with those judgements.

This is not to say, though, that there is no place for 'gut feeling' and intuition. I cannot imagine anybody suggesting that running a business based purely on guesswork and vague impressions is a good idea. Equally, basing every action and decision on detailed analysis can lead to a culture in which nothing is decided without detailed studies that bog the organization down in unnecessary bureaucracy. (Note, however, that it is only *unnecessary* bureaucracy that is bad: bureaucracy has proven to be the most efficient form of government; it is only a problem when it becomes excessive.) Certainly many business success stories are populated with entrepreneurs who *knew* that there was an opportunity and then backed up their intuitive feeling with some research before proceeding.

The same is true for any programme that is aimed at measuring people. We should not ignore those areas of personal performance and interaction that we feel are important just because they did not arise from our first analysis. Similarly, even some of our measurements may come, at least partially, from an understanding of what is going on rather than from some paperwork exercise. An example of this occurred when I was working as a consultant with a small company; a simple internal survey revealed only petty concerns amongst the workforce such as the existence of only one ladies' toilet and the age and reliability of the photocopier. Yet there was a feeling of general unease in the place that was not explained by such trivial concerns and subsequent conversations revealed that everybody was frightened of the owner/manager's temper and, of course, did not feel able to say so in a survey which the owner/manger himself would read! Understanding the exact nature of this problem and how to deal with it obviously required a more formal approach, but it was initially unveiled because somebody *felt* that something was wrong.

After all, intuition is just a way in which our mind processes data and draws conclusions; it is mysterious only because we have an imperfect understanding of how the process works and we therefore mistrust it. It is, however, a valid source of input data to our measurement programme. To ignore such an important and creative input would be to diminish our overall chances of achieving the best that we can from our efforts.

SUMMARY

- The effective use of people is fundamental to any business.
- People need to be managed in a way that provides for a mixture of discipline and freedom.
- We need to measure those factors that directly relate to what we hope for in our people.
- This type of measurement should be generally illustrative and should be distinguished from any personal performance appraisal issues.
- A systems approach helps to us understand how people interface with organizational processes.
- Simple statistical concepts such as mean and range can be useful for interpreting data.
- We can think of the aspects that we wish to measure as being classified as foundation, fuel, results and support.
- Measurements should be aligned to key success factors that underpin the long-term success of the enterprise, and primary concerns, which are today's short-term critical issues.
- We need to measure how people react to the organization but must also understand that the organization has some reaction to its people.
- Formal techniques for identifying what to measure are useful, but we should not ignore our intuition.

CHAPTER THREE

Creating the Right Conditions

USING OBJECTIVITY

'Management by facts and data' is a battle cry that is often heard from organizations that are seeking to establish world-class operations. Whilst many of us might argue that truly successful businesses are also led by intuition and recognition of people's feelings, it is hard to disagree with the point of view that we should rely on evidence rather than on guesswork. After all, it is taking a big risk to guess how well our staff will react, or are reacting, to a change or event rather than do something to try and measure it. If, for example, we mistakenly assume that people are feeling upbeat and will not react too negatively to major change, the outcome could be less of a success than we had hoped.

A key factor affecting objectivity is the way in which an individual might interpret circumstances. Regardless of how systematically data is gathered, there is a danger of employing methods, tools and interpretations that give a personal and non-objective slant to the outcomes. Most of us have views, experiences and opinions that colour our perceptions, and a lack of objectivity can completely ruin any attempt to make decisions based on facts rather than assumptions. Such personal perceptions can be influenced by some apparently irrelevant factors. I have met, for example, managers whose opinions of their staff are partly based on such trivial observations as to what type of drink they order at the bar, what make of vehicle they drive, their sporting allegiances or where they were educated. There also remains a small minority who allow traditional prejudices based on race, gender, age or religion to influence how they feel about people, even though these prejudices are officially taboo. Maintaining the value of the measurements as high as possible therefore requires ways of evaluating people that avoid any trivial or traditional prejudices.

Subjectivity and guesswork are undesirable not only because they can lead to misunderstanding and error, but also because they make our conclusions hard to justify to others. Decisions based on personal preferences ('I like her because we always seem to see the funny side of things together') may feel right at the time but tend to fall apart when subjected to any external scrutiny. This is particularly true if those doing the scrutinizing (managers, employee representatives, customers, colleagues, auditors and so on) do not share the same personal preferences.

What we need are methods that enable us to look at what we think of our people without hindrance from our own petty bigotries. One of the prime areas in which I have seen the importance of this is recruitment. So many times I have seen good internal candidates rejected for a promotion out of hand, thanks to one remembered incident or characteristic. Because the candidate is well-known to us it is easy to remember one error that they made years ago or one aspect of their behaviour that we personally dislike. So our response is to go to great expense to recruit externally and bring in somebody that we hardly know (their performance in a simple interview or even in a prolonged assessment process is no real indication of how they will behave under 'normal' circumstances). What is needed is a sensible approach that tries to make a clear evaluation avoiding unreasonable and unfair judgements.

The typical small company that is considering appointing a line manager to replace the existing incumbent may well reject several internal candidates. Factors such as occasional lateness, a remembered expensive error, recommendations of the departing incumbent (who will probably suggest somebody who will continue in the same style, rather than the 'best' person), a tendency to leave 'on the bell' or failure to participate in social events could all rule somebody out of consideration for the job. This is arbitrary and may unnecessarily lead to the expense and complication of external recruitment.

A better approach would be to apply some of what we have discussed so far. A first step for the recruitment team might be to define their objectives: what do they want from the job and the person that fills it? If we take the example of a managerial position, the objectives could be something like:

- to motivate the department's employees
- to ensure that the normal weekly workload is completed painlessly and cost-effectively
- to cope adequately with crises and workload peaks
- to make best use of financial and other resources
- to continuously improve operations
- to liaise effectively with other functions.

The actual list could be a little longer and more specific than this, but it represents the general idea. The objectives are generated independently of any consideration of existing candidates. Once we know what we are seeking to achieve, then we can try to rate each of the internal candidates against those criteria. There is nothing in the list about always working late, so that should not preclude the candidate who always leaves on time; indeed, he may meet the objectives well since being able to leave on time probably indicates that he is coping comfortably with the daily workload and has the capacity to cope with crises (I am always suspicious of anyone who constantly works very long hours – it often means that they cannot really cope with their work). The candidate who made a previous mistake is also no longer ruled out, since we do not have a criterion that they must never make an error – indeed, to do so would be to rule out everybody who ever lived. In fact we should probably look at how well she has checked her work since the error and view this as a capacity to learn and improve. The only candidates that would now be ruled out are those who have consistently failed to perform adequately in their job in the past.

Next, we can decide whether we have enough internal candidates to provide a fair sample, or whether we would also like to compare them with some potential managers from outside. For this, a method needs to be devised for comparing the attributes of external candidates with our list of objectives. We are then likely to make a far better choice.

This is important. If we believe that it is people who make our business successful, then making the right appointments is fundamental. Choosing somebody on the basis of whether they are a 'good chap' or because they drink alco-pops makes very little sense.

THE NEED TO RETAIN FEELINGS AND IMPRESSIONS

COMBINING SYSTEMS AND EMOTIONS

I already have a picture of a few readers wrinkling their noses with scepticism. 'Surely,' they are saying, 'the truly great organizations are led by people with a sparkle in their eyes and fire in their bellies, not by those who make lists?'

This is largely true. The reason why I have said that people are at the heart of success is that human beings are wonderfully adaptable and creative resources. They can achieve things that no slick process or automated system can. One of the reasons why they are able to do this is their ability to react intuitively to situations, based on their feelings. Yes, they can be programmed to perform some tasks automatically (consider the way in which the subconscious mind performs the basics of driving a car) but, even then, they will make higher-level roadway decisions based on what their judgement tells them to be right at the time.

To suggest, then, that we move to a regime of managing by facts and data alone, excluding the potential for human creativity, would be nonsense. Yet, it would be equally ridiculous to suggest that we can manage by emotions alone. Let us look again at the example of driving a car. A naturally cautious person is likely to drive more safely than a rash one. They are likely to look at the lorry ahead of them wobbling in high cross-winds and decide not to overtake it yet, whereas the rash person may try to pass it at a dangerous time. However, the naturally careful driver will still have accidents if they do not know and follow the detailed rules laid down about which side of the road to use, what to do at junctions, traffic lights and roundabouts, and how to interpret road signs.

The best approach is always to have a good balance. If we can obtain and understand data and learn how to analyse it correctly, we can use that objective information to support our intuitive decisions. To ignore one aspect or the other is to ignore some of the resources at our disposal.

THE RESULTS OF INTERACTIONS

Another way in which we must ensure that we are taking account of feelings and emotions is in the impact that our actions and decisions have on people. There is a danger that any programme aiming to put more rigour into our dealings with people will concentrate on 'hard' issues such as efficiency, allied with corporate objectives and personal effectiveness. We must remember, though, that people are affected personally by what goes on in the workplace. What may seem like a good basis for a decision today, because it is based on objective evidence, could ultimately fall apart if it is so unpopular that employees become demotivated and dispirited. How the team will react emotionally to our decisions is just as important as the technical changes that the decision represents.

This is not to say that we must never do anything to upset anybody. Sometimes hard, unpopular business decisions are necessary. When we need to take such decisions, however, we still need to understand how people are feeling now, what the emotional effects of previous decisions and events have been and how they are likely to feel when the new decision is announced. If we understand this well enough it can aid our decision-making process. Given that unwelcome changes are necessary, are there ways of implementing it that will allay some of the worst fears of the workforce or take care of the issues that they are most concerned about or ameliorate any negative reaction? If we know how people will feel about what happens, rather than just look at the more 'technical' implications, we will be able to make decisions that achieve their aims but minimize negative repercussions.

I am not advocating a cynical approach that uses an awareness of people's feelings to manipulate them but, rather, suggesting that by appreciating what people want (and what they do not know they want but we can determine that they are affected by) we can help meet their needs and address their concerns. Changes and developments that are thus handled in a sympathetic manner will make life better for the employees and, at the same time, allow our plans to progress more smoothly.

UNDERSTANDING INDIVIDUALITY

In the recruitment scenario described above, the company was looking for a single person to fill a role and would therefore naturally look at the individual characteristics of each candidate. Consider, however, a situation where the customer support function of a company is trying to set up a new team. They have a help-desk that takes and tracks the calls, as well as a field service unit that employs engineers to fix technical problems at customer premises. They are now looking, though, to establish a new section that sits somewhere between the two, that will take calls that cannot be answered by reference to the frequently asked questions (FAQ) list but for which a site visit would represent an unreasonable expense. They could, for example, simulate and investigate an intermittent fault seen by an overseas customer that does not prevent their equipment from functioning but only occurs sporadically and may not be witnessed by a visiting service technician.

In such a case it is harder to define a single set of objectives and 'score' the candidate for appointment to the team against them. If we did that, we would end up with a team made up of virtually identical people. Although there may be characteristics that we would expect all members of such a group to have in common, we would also need a mix of abilities to enable the team to perform well together and cover all activities needed within the new department. Having a team composed of a group that all have the same skill-sets would inevitably lead to conflict in some areas, with others being ignored. Bearing this in mind is also important for maintaining the long-term viability of a measurement programme, as discussed in Chapter Eleven.

In such cases we cannot specify a single set of characteristics that we are seeking and aim to match every candidate to them; we can make sure that our overall objectives are met by the group as a whole. This requires an integrated recruitment approach, rather than considering each candidate as an individual.

This factor leads us to consider how we will deal with measuring people who are intrinsically different. It is impossible to measure individual people and hope to obtain the results that we seek; we must measure the group as a whole, or at least a representative sample. From these measurements we can then determine whether the group as a whole is displaying the characteristics and behaviour that we expect. Such a process can never be used, however, as a tool for allocating individual blame. For the same reasons, it does not lend itself to providing information for personal and individual performance appraisal. Nevertheless, what we should be able to see is how the overall workforce or team responds to the current or changing situation, enabling the organization to tailor its approach to achieve the most in terms of loyalty, commitment, effort and motivation.

COPING WITH DIVERSITY

However, just because we have recognized that a range of opinions and attitudes is valuable, this does not mean that it is easy to deal with. The first thing that we have to appreciate is that different viewpoints will necessarily entail occasional disagreement. We have to accept that others will have objections to our ideas that had not previously occurred to us and, equally, will see merits in other ideas that we had not considered. Our natural tendency, however, is to seek the confirmation of like-minded people. When I was responsible for diversification at a telecommunications company, I used to seek out a particular engineering project manager when I wished to discuss new prospects, since I knew that he and I shared a common outlook and that he would be much more likely to support my ideas than reject them. This made life easy and comfortable for me because he never challenged anything fundamental about my ideas; as he was fully in tune with my own guiding principles, any adverse comments were never directed at anything other than minor details.

We must learn not to do this. First, we must accept the idea that multiple and varied inputs to all facets of running an organization make for a more successful operation. Second, we should educate ourselves to seek a wide range of inputs on all occasions. Third, we need to learn not to think of viewpoints that differ from our own as wrong – merely as extra input.

DIVERSITY IN MEASUREMENT

If we relate these ideas to those of introducing some objectivity to our evaluations of people, there are a number of steps that we can take to embed the concepts of diversity in our measurements. The first step is to identify the types of diverse feeling or opinion that we might encounter.

I have often worked with organizations on the introduction of operating and procedure manuals. Doing this well can be a tricky task, with the emphasis often falling on the technical and operational aspects of the 'rule book' rather than on how it will affect the people that have to use or follow it. I did, however, once work on a project where the human resources manager was tasked with overseeing the project. She had seen a number of styles and designs of such manuals and wanted to be sure that the organization chose that which worked best for them. She distilled the basics of each style into a simple description and then discussed with the staff what they did and did not like in order to find out how people felt about such documents. As a result, she drew up the following list:

- Some like pictures better than words.
- Some are irritated by poor grammar and jargon.
- Some insist that they cannot read any long documents on a computer screen.
- Some like detailed explanations of the reasons behind any instruction.
- Some have a natural distrust of any written instruction.
- Some want every step spelt out to the tiniest detail.

In addition, of course, some just did not care about any one of these. Having elicited an understanding of the broad feelings of the work team, the HR manager then looked at the style options available to her and considered how they might cater to, or irritate, the feelings of the team. From this she was able to choose a style that met her own needs yet also broadly met the mood of the target audience. In some cases, where the selected format was likely to run counter to some work-group preferences, she was able to think of ways to ameliorate the effects.

Once we know the range of different feelings and opinions held by our people, we are in a position not only to tailor our actions to their preferences, but also to put them to a second purpose, that of direct measurement. We can set up audits or measures to monitor to what extent each of these feelings is being experienced and expressed within the organization, or we can measure how well any new initiative is addressing those concerns. This is especially useful when a change occurs, whether externally or internally initiated. The important thing is to look for the right balance in those measurements, not just determining how well any initiative meets a manager's primary objective.

USING IMPRESSIONS CONSTRUCTIVELY

I spent part of my career teaching people how to conduct quality audits. This is a technique of examining the processes in an organization and seeing how well their operation is capable of meeting requirements such as customer contracts, specifications, quality standards, corporate objectives and process operating manuals. Such auditors – particularly those whose role is to recommend awards or certificates – are taught that they should never report anything based on impressions, which could be mistaken, but only on objective evidence. Whilst this might be appropriate for some activities such as legal adjudication, examination scoring or technical testing (we would be alarmed if a regulatory chief approved a new drug for use because he 'had a good feeling about it'), it is not necessarily appropriate for those aiming to create a high-performance culture. Managers *are* involved; they do not need to pretend to any form of aloof detachment. Their opinions and impressions, as well as those of the people around them, are an integral part of the running of the organization.

THE MANAGER'S IMPRESSIONS

The first way in which impressions can be used is by the person who is controlling a process, project or initiative. Their overall impressions about how well something is going can be as valuable as some of the process measurements that indicate the current status of the operational aspects of work; just because we have achieved our output targets today does not mean that we will do so tomorrow since we may only have attained our current level of success through an initial spurt of energy or by generating high stress levels amongst those involved.

It is important to be active and systematic in the use of impressions. Quick, off-the-cuff evaluations with little forethought are dangerous. These are typified by the scenario in which someone pokes their head around the team leader's office door, asking whether the team are keen to start their new project, and the team leader gives a gut-reaction response without having even considered the question before. In such cases, the response will usually be led the way in which the question is phrased: 'I expect your team are looking forward to the new project, aren't they?' would probably elicit a positive response, whereas it would be very to hard to answer with anything other than 'Not too badly, considering' if asked 'And how did the team take that bombshell, then?'.

The professional approach, aimed at obtaining objective results, is to consider carefully and proactively what our impressions are and confirm them by testing them at regular intervals. Then, when we need to use the answers to questions or plan future actions, we will be ready with an accurate analysis, avoiding the quick conclusion that may lead others to false assumptions. It is even better if we can, as described earlier in this chapter, consider what categories of impressions we would typically have in various business situations and consider how strong each is at key times, such as when coping with a large project or change initiative.

A good approach is to list the overall impressions that we have had in the past, add a few that we are feeling at the moment which have, perhaps, not cropped up before and then allocate a score against each one. We can do this simply by sitting quietly and asking ourselves how strong is our impression in each area and allocating a value, say, from zero to five. Five might indicate that it is a strong impression, one is weak and zero means that we do not have that impression at all on this occasion – for example, it might be usual for new employees to be treated with suspicion, the level of which could be ranked in each case; if, then, on one occasion, a recruit was immediately taken into the bosom of the work team, the score would be given as zero. We will explore this theme of scoring in more detail throughout the rest of this book.

As a basic measurement system this approach could be used simply as it is. If a leader regularly scores their impressions on a defined list of topics and plots the answers, they may obtain some indication of how things are changing. Of course, this is rather subjective and is, obviously, rather less sophisticated than the other techniques described in subsequent chapters, but it can provide a good starting point, especially in smaller organizations, as long as the recommendations for analysis and action found in this book are adopted.

OTHER'S PEOPLE'S IMPRESSIONS

Although other people's impressions are more varied (particularly in a large work-group) and are harder to discern, they can also be categorized. We can then apply the same system of scoring. In this case, the score may have to be an average of what the whole team feels, but since these scores are relatively arbitrary anyway this is not really a problem. If you wish to reflect the fact that there are a number of different attitudes yet still wish to keep the analysis relatively simple, you could include another column on your sheet of paper showing the range (the difference between the highs and lowest score for all members of the team, as described in Chapter Two). An illustration of how this might work is given in Table 3.1.

Table 3.1   Measurement results with means and ranges

Aspect	Mean	Range
Timekeeping	7	4
Distraction	5	5
Loitering	6	8
Telephone manner	8	2
Policy understanding	6	8
Team loyalty	8	3
Company loyalty	7	5
Thrift	9	2
Grumbling	7	7
Social involvement	6	9

BEING CONSTRUCTIVE

It is essential to remember that the only reason for monitoring feelings and impressions is to do something constructive with them. If we appreciate the need for diversity, there is no excuse for using the information to decide which members of the team we are happy with and which we are not. Indeed, if we use our analysis of feelings and impressions for this purpose then we will quickly find that our sources of information dry up as people realize that their revelations are being used against them. Furthermore, as we have already ascertained that these measurements are not suitable for individual appraisal, we would not run the risk of using the data in a way that produces invalid conclusions.

On the other hand, if we believe that we have a good idea of the range of opinions that are likely to be found, measurements of what people are actually feeling will allow us to see whether we are going in the right direction and enable us to do something about it if not. For example, if we expect at least half the team to be nervous about a new initiative but, when we measure, we find that none of them feels this way, it could indicate that we have done a good job in selling the change, but it is more likely to suggest that we have not explained the changes fully enough with the result that people have not yet fully grasped their full extent. Equally, if analysis and consideration reveal that people really are more accepting than we had believed, it would allow us to proceed with changes faster or more extensively than we had planned. And if we find that they are even more nervous than we had feared, then this also may lead us to proceed even more gently.

Similarly, by trying to find out what people are feeling we can see whether or not our plans are proceeding as expected. A solid investigation of what people are thinking might reveal, for instance, that it is commonly believed that recent developments have only taken place because the company is gearing itself up to be sold to a competitor, whereas in fact the scheme is intended to directly combat the competition. Knowing that such feelings exist, and how strongly, can be far more useful if determined actively when there is time to consider their implications than to discover them at an angry staff meeting.

Such information can also be used for counselling and coaching. Again, we can make sure that we do not wait until the feelings of a group or team start to affect their performance but can take steps to find out why they exist and do something to ameliorate any negative effects.

JUSTIFYING CONCLUSIONS

I have said that we must try to be rigorous in understanding any issues related to people because off-the-cuff conclusions are dangerous. What can represent an even greater danger, though, is thinking that we have all the answers and have drawn the right conclusions just because we have written something down on a check sheet rather than simply thought of it. The very fact that we have created a list of feelings and put a number against them carries the risk of giving them too much strength and credibility, making it even more important to properly and systematically justify our conclusions to eliminate any misconceptions and misunderstandings.

It is also important to understand that there is no absolute 'right' answer to any consideration of how people feel. True, we may be able to judge whether somebody feels good or bad about something (although even that is complicated – my 12-year-old daughter cried when she had her dental brace fitted but also wanted the tidy smile that it would eventually bring and was secretly pleased at the thought that it made her look like a 'real teenager'), but we are on shakier ground when determining exactly how strongly they feel.

Although the techniques and attitudes adopted by scientists and engineers are often derided as too cold and analytical by those more closely involved with the intricacies of people-based processes, it is necessary to adopt some of the methods that typify the scientific approach when trying to employ any form of people-based measurement. We need to be sure that we fully understand what we are measuring, how it will be enumerated, against what accepted scale the measurement will be reported and how the results will be compared against empirical or equivalent data. In other words, we must have some reasonably scientific means of allocating our resultant scores.

This implies that the score we allocate to each impression or feeling must be repeatable. If we conduct an evaluation today and then conduct it again one month later under identical circumstances we should be able to report exactly the same results. In practice, our objectivity and adherence to the scientific principle will not be verifiable since, in real situations, circumstances and feelings do not remain constant for long enough for repeatability to be confirmed. This does not mean, however, that we can ignore the need. If we do not 'calibrate' our measurement technique to make it as repeatable as possible, then we will have no idea whether an indicated change results from a real change or simply from a poor measurement.

REMOVING DOUBT AND SUSPICION

Most management initiatives and developments are treated with at least some suspicion by the workforce. At best, they worry that any accompanying changes will make their jobs harder, more time-consuming or less secure. At worst, they imagine them to be a sinister plot to undermine the entire foundation of their livelihood. This sort of attitude can exist even where the programme covers something relatively impersonal such as information technology or capital equipment. When the new initiative directly involves the study of people, then the reactions of those involved could well be extremely negative.

Such reactions can have an impact on the very things that we are trying to measure. If we suddenly announce, for instance, that we are going to be measuring employee morale and allocating a percentage score to it, this may cause sufficient fear and suspicion to cause morale to drop. Announcing the low results of our measurement will then indicate that morale is low causing people to worry and making morale fall even further. Although the ultimate aim of measuring anything should be to help us make changes, we should not create changes that are unintended and certainly not in a direction opposite to that which we desire.

The answer to this is to communicate. We must make it absolutely clear to everybody that we are measuring to improve the way in which the organization is managed and that it is not a way to create a new stick with which to beat them. The best approach is to start telling people when we first start to think about it, well before we actually design and implement our measurements. Then the same message needs to be regularly reinforced and clarified, so that, by the time we start measuring and using the data to make changes, everyone will be so familiar with the idea that it will come as no shock and will not appear threatening.

> **TIP**
> This is the right approach for *any* change; talk about it at length before implementation and when it comes it will be much more readily accepted.

OPENNESS AND INTEGRITY

If we accept that strong communication is one of the facets of a successful programme, then it should follow that anybody wanting to take the measurement of people seriously must develop a culture of openness. Not only should we tell our workforce that we are going to measure them and that they do not need to worry, but we must explain the details of what we are doing and provide them with access to those details. This does not mean that we need to gather everybody in a lecture theatre and take them through in detail how the figures are calculated, like a class of 15-year-olds studying quadratic equations (since they will often be just as uninterested in this topic as the teenagers are in theirs), but we do need to make everything accessible to the people being measured if they express an interest. Exactly what we will measure, how the data will be analysed and who will act upon the results must be 'in the public domain'.

PUBLISHING THE RESULTS

Taking this commitment to openness seriously means publishing any results and analyses widely. There is absolutely no point in trying to convince people of our good intentions by appraising them of the process if we do not share the outputs of that process.

Now, I must confess that my natural reaction to my own suggestion of widely publishing all results is to feel a little nervous. After all, propaganda, even of the internal variety, can be a powerful weapon. What if the measurements show poor results? Will that have a negative impact on morale? Say, for example, our analyses show that the sales and marketing department has no confidence in the company's future. Since that function is in the best place to foresee forward sales and market share, the rest of the workforce are likely to take such pessimism as a prompt to desert the ship. Even worse, what happens if the media or the competition gets to hear that we have some proven weaknesses? Even though our competitors may have just as many faults as we do, if they are not directly measuring theirs they can rightly say that they have not discovered any flaws as bad as ours. Customers, too, might take a dim view and decide that any weaknesses revealed represent too great a risk. Although such reactions to improvement efforts are unreasonable, they are certainly quite a common fear amongst managers who worry that a tool for their own use could easily become a weapon to be used against them.

These fears, although they are part of my own gut reaction, do not, of course, represent my considered view. They are typically a sign of a manager's own uncertainty and human frailty rather than of their intellectual capacity. We will need to overcome these fears and 'sell' the benefits to the leaders of the organization as well as to the workforce at large. Once the need and benefits are explained, many of the fears will be put to rest, although one should expect some lingering concerns that can only be assuaged by proving that the overall programme works and has more benefits than drawbacks.

To illustrate the point, we can draw a parallel here with medical information. In the early part of the twentieth century, physicians judged that patients were too ignorant to understand what was wrong with them and that most things should be hidden from them so as not to alarm them. Today, we consider such attitudes as patronizing and harmful. Modern doctors are more likely to be chastised for withholding information than for providing too much.

Much of this is about showing that we have integrity. If we really intend our measurements of people to be constructive, positive and blame-free, then we should stick by this at all times, even when it feels slightly uncomfortable to do so. If we say that we are going to tell people what we are doing and what progress we are making then we must always keep our promises. If we say that it is not personal, then we must ensure that the programme is never misused (however tempting it might be, sometimes, to use information to further some mildly unworthy motive or simply not to take some action because we are a bit busy).

SUMMARY

- Managing by facts and data is generally preferable to relying on guesswork.
- Facts and data can also help eliminate subjectivity and prejudice.
- Using a systematic approach can help improve the effectiveness of most tasks that deal with people.
- Feelings are important, though; they should not be excluded from our considerations.
- People's feelings and behaviours will be affected by what is happening around them as well as by their natural inclinations.
- There is an element of individual input into measurement results, although people measurements should not be confused with personal performance appraisal.
- Different people will react differently to situations and we must allow for diversity in our thinking.
- Any measurement and analysis must lead to a constructive outcome and must not be used as a reason to complain or blame.
- Conclusions reached from measurements should be justifiable and based on systematic processes.
- These processes should also be designed to be as objective as possible.
- People may be suspicious about being measured; objectivity and open communication are ways of dealing with this.
- Integrity and lack of secrecy are also key elements in creating trust in, and support for, a measurement programme.

CHAPTER FOUR

Choosing the Measurements

WHAT TO MEASURE

Knowing exactly what to measure in any given circumstance or organization is perhaps the most fundamental, and the most difficult, of the activities involved in setting up a people measurement programme. Although it would have been splendid to be able to remove that difficulty for readers by listing those elements that have been shown to be the best to measure, the immensely varied nature of organizations and their staffing make that impossible.

Instead, we need to understand how the various factors influencing and dependent on our people interact with each other and the business as a whole, and then make our decisions on the basis of that knowledge. In Chapter Two we discussed the categorization of people aspects and looked at key success factors (KSFs) and current primary concerns, and we can use these concepts to help us determine what people factors exist and which ones we most wish to measure.

> TIP
> It can be a good idea to have several key people, such as members of the measurement team, conduct the analysis of what to measure separately. First, hold a simple meeting to introduce the scheme and then give each participant a sheet with standard headings and ask them to list what they would measure under each one. A comparison of the lists will reveal those items identified by every participant as being of major interest, but will also allow others to consider good ideas that they had not so far thought of.

An initial set of factors to measure created by the human resources manager of a small industrial company was:

- punctuality
- loyalty to the company and the management hierarchy
- compliance (measured by the number of times that employees had to be disciplined for breach of rules or policy)
- willingness (that is, whether or not people refused to work late, travel, alter their arrangements and so on when asked)
- length of service
- cheerfulness.

Not surprisingly, some of these are more difficult to measure than others. The list also covers a range of topics, from those directly affecting performance to some, such as cheerfulness, which are desirable but with a less direct impact on everyday work. What is striking about this list, though, is that it is clearly devised from the company management viewpoint. Traditionally, managers expect their staff to demonstrate attributes that will directly benefit the organization and spend time making sure that their team possesses those attributes, rewarding those members who display them most strongly and admonishing those who adhere to them less well than expected.

This is, however, too narrow a viewpoint. It is one-sided. Obtaining the best from people necessitates addressing their needs as well as those of the corporation. In the same way that military commanders understand the need for a well-fed fighting force, so commercial leaders should be aiming to feed the inner person as well as looking for desirable outputs. This means that the things we should measure should relate just as much to how well the company is treating the workers as to how well the workers perform for the company.

Loyalty, for example, should work two ways. Just as we do not expect our employees to denigrate our products and services when drinking coffee with their friends, so managers of the organization should not speak badly of individuals or groups to those outside or even to other internal groups. My wife often puts this idea into words when expressing her family loyalty. 'I can say what I like about my relatives,' she says, 'but woe betide anyone else who criticizes them.'

So the HR manager should perhaps have made two lists, under the headings of 'worker to organization' and 'organization to worker'. The first list may well be the set of items shown earlier. The second could include, for example:

- communication
- recognition (praise given for success or effort)
- perceived equality and fairness
- consistency and planning
- support and flexibility (the effort that the management makes to make allowance for personal difficulties, short-term problems and so on).

This would have broadened the focus from simply thinking about what we expect from our employees to what employees expect of us. In most cases, this is not as easy as for the ancient military commander who might have considered that troops were being well treated as long as they were being well fed and not beaten too often. Modern business expects that the workforce is well treated and respected, so that quantifying how well we do this must be part of any good measurement regime. Whether this bidirectional approach arises from the realization that more will be gained from people if they are treated well or from an altruistic vision that people should be considered as more than mere work units in immaterial for the purposes of the exercise, as long as it is understood that the programme must be balanced to avoid suspicion and resentment amongst those being measured.

THE BENEFITS OF GOOD SELECTION

One danger when embarking on any form of measurement programme is that we become grateful that we have found anything at all that we are able to measure. For many of us, recording and analysing our performance is both intellectually and operationally difficult – intellectually because it can feel uncomfortable if it shows us in a bad light, and operationally because it is time-consuming and takes us away from 'doing', which we see as being our main objective. This often results in our first measurement selections arising from the question 'What can I measure?' rather than the more correct 'What should I measure?'

In some circumstances, this need not be a major problem. The fact that we are measuring anything at all is at least a start; we can modify and improve the way in which we do it as time goes on. This avoids the risk of spending so much time trying to make it right before we begin that we never actually get the process off the ground. When dealing with people, however, we need to take more care. If we are measuring something operational, such as oven temperature, and we then find that this is not the most important product characteristic and we would be better off measuring something else, then all we have lost is a little time and effort. If, however, we begin measuring something personal then we create an expectation amongst the workforce that something will be done with that data; if we then decide we do not want to use the information gathered we create disillusionment and a lack of willingness to cooperate in future.

This, then, is one of the first pairs of benefits of selecting our measurement parameters well: that we do not have to substantially change what we measure after early trials and that we thus maintain the goodwill of the people being monitored. This also leads into another bonus of choosing the right things: perceived image. If we choose the types of measurement suggested by the HR manager earlier, the workforce may well perceive that the programme is being put in place to grind them down. Even worse, they may believe that its purpose is to weed out unsatisfactory workers and find evidence for their dismissal; terror has been a tactic used by many leaders in the past. People will never give of their best if they are living in fear; a programme that is seen to support workers will go a long way towards eliminating such fear.

By carefully considering what we are going to measure and allowing suitable debate and selection we will, of course, reap all the usual benefits of good planning. These include avoiding having to redo the exercise, knowing what we are doing and making overall success more likely. There is also the less obvious benefit of confidence. If we have done sufficient planning to understand what we are going to do and are sure that we have selected the right measurements, we will be much more confident when trying to sell the programme to others.

BEHAVIOURS

When we are considering personal, rather than operational, measurements we have to think about what we can really enumerate and what constitutes meaningful analysis. Are we, for example, interested in underlying beliefs and opinions? Or are we more interested in what people do than what they feel? A parallel to this can be found in some religious debates; older and more traditional faiths tend to have strong emphasis on following a set of rules and conformance to defined ritual, whereas some newer branches feel that personal faith is more important than formal observance. Just as each devotee pursues the path that is most appropriate to their beliefs, so in our organization we may feel that we do not mind what people secretly feel as long as they follow corporate policy, or on the other hand (perhaps in a creative environment, for example, where we need more emotional commitment from our employees) it may be useful to try to understand how people feel.

We can decide, then, where our emphasis lies. Are we worried about what people feel in private and mumble to their spouses at night, or are we more concerned with what they actually do? One may have an impact upon the other, but could be completely hidden under a veneer of company loyalty.

I tend to believe that, in any but the most exceptional cases, behaviours are more important than inner feelings or beliefs. This is for a number of reasons:

● It can be argued that nobody cares what a person thinks as long as they continue to perform well (a cynical view but with some validity).

- Behaviours can be measured, whereas feelings present a little more difficulty.
- Feelings do not contribute to corporate performance, whereas behaviour does.

I also subscribe to the 'arranged marriage' point of view. Arranged marriages often work because the couple accept the principle of having to cooperate closely and live together as wife and husband, so that, after a time, the act becomes so familiar that it is what they desire and an inseparable bond is formed. Thus, arranged marriages can be a success even though believing that the best choice has been made may only come some time after the choice itself. The same can be true of behaviour at work. If people act and behave in a certain way for long enough, that behaviour becomes normal and people begin to believe in what they are doing. In this way, external appearance can become internal conviction. In reality, this is just as likely to be the reason for success as when people decide to act in a certain way because of deeply held beliefs. Indeed, we often find that those who may seem to be reluctantly following a path in the early days because of some personal opinion will quickly become converts; it will only be the most extremely held convictions that prevent compliance to the edicts of authority. If the convictions of our people are not extremely held (and by definition of the word 'extreme' such beliefs are rare), they are certainly less important than what those people actually do. So, for example, managers do not have to believe in their hearts that expenditure restraint is important, as long as they do keep their costs down; staff may not really see why the company expects mutual courtesy in the workplace but this does not matter as long as they practise it. When we are designing measurements, therefore, we must keep in mind what we really need from the workforce and measure that, rather than what we might believe altruistically that they should feel.

BEHAVIOURAL LINKS

One behaviour, or set of behaviours, often has an impact on others. For example, leading a team well depends partly on being a good communicator. So if we are studying behaviours in a leader, and we are particularly interested in how well they lead a team, we would probably need to measure communication in addition to other factors such as discipline, planning and so on. This has a number of implications for how and what we measure:

- We must identify all the factors that interact and measure them all – or, if not all, at least the strongest of them. If we only measure a sample of them, we are likely to miss out on important information. It is all very well to monitor overall employee satisfaction but, if the index falls, we would need more detailed information on which particular areas have caused the dissatisfaction (it may, for instance, be just one apparently trivial thing that is easy to solve but is having a disproportionate effect on the feelings of our people).
- By measuring all the interacting elements we are better able to analyse our results and hence target our corrective or improvement actions.
- We need to identify and monitor areas of balance. For example, we may desire enthusiasm amongst our workers so could attempt to measure it; however, enthusiastic people often allow new ideas to distract them from their current work, so we may also need to measure 'focus' or the ability to complete a task to keep the balance. As there is always a danger of concentrating on measured performance areas at the expense of other linked factors, the measurement programme must take account of all the important and most desired people performance elements.

Part of our process of knowing what to measure should be to identify sets and balanced opposites of factors in which we are interested. When we have decided what we intend to measure it is useful to define which factors are dependent on which others. This helps make sense of what is happening when we come to analyse the results.

BEHAVIOURAL HIERARCHIES

Different behaviours may also be linked hierarchically. When considering what we wish for amongst our staff we may well initially identify an all-encompassing concept to measure such as loyalty, since loyal employees will channel their energies into the company's interests and should be much more productive. When we start to consider what we actually mean by 'loyalty', however, we may discover that we are looking for something more specific – for instance, faith in corporate polices and support of the overall ethos. We can then consider in turn what we really mean by these – for example, faith in corporate polices might be revealed by adherence to them and the extent to which they are referred to in daily work. Now that we have 'drilled down' to a lower level we have things that are measurable; adherence to policies can be measured by supervision and audit, and access to policy statements can be monitored via the IT system that controls access to the appropriate section of the intranet.

Thus, managers may still want a 'loyalty' index, but the way in which they measure loyalty could be by looking at behaviours linked hierarchically to that criterion.

Equally, we can look at the picture the other way around. It is possible, for example, to measure how often objections are raised to new policies or instructions, but we need to decide what that tells us – is it due to the level of anarchy present in the workforce or does it more truly indicate an intelligent ability to analyse and question? In fact, the 'What does it reveal?' test is an excellent one for many measurements. If we have something that we can quantify, but we are not sure what the numbers mean, we may have chosen the wrong measurement or fallen into the trap of selecting something that can be measured rather than trying to measure things that tell us what we want to know. A full and thorough analysis of results and their meaning is critical to deciding what to do about any measurement indicators.

EFFECTS ON PROCESSES

For the most part, there are appreciable differences between measurements of people factors and measurements of processes in that process measurements are often more straightforward. There are, however, links between the two. Since any but the most automated processes have some human input, it follows that any human factors that are worth measuring will also have an impact on process results.

We can use this fact to provide yet another means of identifying which people factors we wish to measure, through looking first at what we wish to achieve from our processes. Process measurements can be identified from the following steps:

1. Understand exactly what the process is that we are considering; what it is for and what its boundaries are.
2. Identify who the customers for the process are. These may be real customers, external to the organization, or internal customers – people within the organization who rely on the actions that this process takes and the items or services that it provides for them in order to be able to perform their own processes satisfactorily.

> **TIP**
>
> Any programme aimed at improving effectiveness and efficiency should include some element of understanding who the internal customers are. This is also true of any initiative aimed at improving the people elements of the business since it helps everybody understand how their own contribution fits into the overall picture.

3. Determine, through analysis and questioning, what the key requirements of all customers are.
4. Identify which process outputs contribute directly to meeting those key requirements.
5. Find a way of quantifying the performance level for each process output that directly relates to customer satisfaction.
6. Set target levels for each of them so that it can be determined whether or not the requirements are actually being met.
7. Using a cause-and-effect analysis, identify upstream process factors that affect the outputs and find ways of measuring them too. Set targets for these in the same way that they were set for the output measurements.
8. Establish a procedure for regularly taking and tracking both output and upstream measurements and comparing them to their target values.
9. Use occasions when upstream targets are not met to instigate action to pull the process back on track before the output targets become endangered.
10. Use occasions when output targets are not met to prompt improvements in the process design and operation to prevent future recurrence of the problem.

If we have taken a detailed and comprehensive approach such as this, it should be easy to find people issues that fit into the model. Analysis of the customer ordering process, for example, may have an output measurement that represents total processing time, with upstream measurements related to the amount of time spent on individual steps in the process. We could then think of personal factors that might influence each of these, contributing to the overall speed and level of service – for example:

- enthusiasm
- energy
- understanding of the principle that the 'customer is king'
- cheerfulness.

Since many organizations now have process or other measurements in place, in order to fit business excellence models, provide information to head office, meet the requirements of standards such as ISO 9001 or ISO 14001, or simply to provide a business management tool, using the existing process measurement framework to identify what people factors might be measured can represent a simple and speedy way of beginning to identify people measurements.

LINKS TO OTHER MEASUREMENTS

FINANCIAL MEASUREMENTS

The most common and popular type of measurement in place in every organization is financial. Everybody measures their income, expenditure, profit and cash position (as an independent businessman I tend to perform an informal cash flow prediction in my head at least twice per day). Many organizations will, of course, have a far wider range of financial measurements that analyse monetary performance in a variety of sophisticated and detailed ways.

Since financial measurements are well understood and practised in all organizations, it might seem a good idea to begin with those and develop associated people factors. Unfortunately they have little in common with measurements of people. Yes, we could argue that, if pay and remuneration are poor, morale will be low but it is widely accepted today that the link between salary and motivation is low; remuneration is a negative driver in that it demotivates if it is too low but increasing it beyond a basic satisfaction threshold does little to increase overall employee morale. In general, those defining what to measure of the organization's people should not start by using financial measurements to provide ideas.

CUSTOMER SATISFACTION

Perhaps the second most popular form of corporate measurement is that of customer satisfaction. This is an idea which is sold strongly by both marketing and quality professionals as well as by business change advisers and consultants. As a result, it has become relatively widespread and its use has increased even further since it became a requirement of the ISO 9001 quality standard in late 2000.

Customer satisfaction depends heavily on how the organization's employees behave. If they are brusque, surly and unhelpful, customer satisfaction will be low. If they are courteous, keen and communicative, satisfaction will be high. This works well for manufacturing and supply industries where buyers require detailed information about the products that they are purchasing and will be delighted if the information (delivery time, specifications, interfaces, shipment methods and so on) is quickly and readily forthcoming and will be upset if they have to struggle to find things out, no matter how good the product itself is. It works twofold for service industries where customer satisfaction is even more dependent on the personal approach of the people with whom the customer deals.

If your organization already measures customer satisfaction, it is certainly worth examining both the data collection and analysis methods and the results. These may give you existing information about the levels of performance of your people, especially if the measurement is more sophisticated than a single index and gives separate data on various aspects of customer satisfaction such as the apparent helpfulness of staff. Indeed, you may find that these already provide some high-level people measurements that you can use unmodified as part of your wider programme.

STRATEGIC VERSUS OPERATIONAL LEVELS

As mentioned in Chapter One, all organizational and business measurements can operate at a variety of levels. They can range from something that reflects the performance of the business as a whole or can be as low-level and detailed as the hours worked by an individual today.

The best known of the high-level, strategic measurements is profit (equating, for non-profit organizations, to adherence to budgets or similar measures). This, as mentioned earlier in this chapter, is part of the financial analysis that every company carries out and is the one measurement with which everybody is familiar. It is intended to define how well the whole organization is doing. It is dependent on the results of every process that the organization carries out, yet may not be particularly sensitive to changes in any one of those processes. Similarly, a change in profit levels may be difficult to attribute to any single factor, especially in large, complex organizations. Thus it is a reasonable measure of what is going on globally, but has limited use as a tool for improvement or personal motivation. Such measurements are of particular interest to senior managers but have only limited relevance for someone trying to manage an internal process.

At the other end of the spectrum is the individual, operational measurement which measures a single aspect of an individual activity. It is highly sensitive to variation of performance within that activity but is not affected, or at least only marginally affected, by anything that goes on outside the process. An example of this might be the number of calls per hour dealt with by a telephone support desk operator; this is affected by the speed of the operator, the design of the tools provided for them and the nature of the query from the customer, all of which are within the process. Whilst external factors, such as the quality of the product, might affect the number of calls being received they have no real impact on the number of calls that the individual is able to handle. These measurements are of interest to those looking to manage the individual person or process and are usually at too detailed a level to be of interest to senior managers. They have the advantage that they are often detailed enough to enable immediate fault-finding if they indicate a problem, but they can fall into the trap of being measured totally in isolation so that good measurement results and good business practice are totally unrelated. Competent design of the measurement programme must be employed to remove this pitfall.

Of course, the types of measurement available are not really polarized into extremes. In fact, they can be relatively strategic but tending towards the detail level, or process-based but with a broader flavour. The measurement continuum given in Figure 1.1 (p. 9) illustrates this. Any one measurement will occupy a small band within that spectrum (not a spot, since measurements of any business characteristics other than the most purely technical will have a complex make-up). People measurements may vary across virtually the whole range, from an individual's specific behaviour to a broad understanding of the feelings of the whole workforce over a protracted period. When we choose something to monitor, it is important to appreciate where in the continuum the measurement lies, since this will dictate the type of action to be taken when required. For instance, a strategic-level indicator showing low performance would necessitate investigation as to the root causes of the problem and establishment of a project to eliminate them, whereas process-level problems may well be resolved by spot action to a predetermined formula, such as giving a short rest break when a front-office employee shows signs of tiredness.

Readers should be aware, though, that practical restraints will mean that very few people measurements will actually lie at the low-level end of the spectrum, simply because, in order to be meaningful, low-level measurements typically have to be immediate and acted upon quickly. As we will discover as we explore the subject more deeply, people measurements typically require careful study, interpretation and analysis and, often, comparisons with more than one set of previous, or baseline, data. This removes much opportunity for immediate remedy.

TIP

Just because low-level people measurements may turn out to be impractical does not mean that the topic is invalid. Something at the detail level which we decide cannot be formally measured may still represent an opportunity for us to devise a less formal way to monitor it.

OBSERVER EFFECTS

When choosing what measurements we are to take and considering how to take them, we must remember the old principle that the observer affects the measurement. This is probably best known in relativistic terms – as Einstein demonstrated, as the speed of light is approached, whoever is taking a measurement affects what is being measured – but it is equally valid in the rather more mundane process of simply monitoring what goes on in our organizations.

Many readers will remember the example (which I first heard in a university lecture entitled 'Operations Research' – a term that seems to have disappeared today) of the factory where lighting levels were changed in an attempt to find the optimum level for worker efficiency. In fact it was found that productivity rose in all areas during the experiment, even when the level of lighting had remained constant! This was because the people knew they were being watched and therefore put in a little more effort.

> **TIP**
> Do not take the above example as an indication that productivity can be improved by introducing tighter direct supervision; experience shows that such improvements, beyond a certain basic level, are temporary and will quickly fade.

When we are directly measuring people factors, rather than process parameters such as productivity, this effect will be even more pronounced, because the people themselves are being studied rather than just something that they are involved in. If productivity changes because people know that it is being studied, then they are certain to react when they know that their personal behaviours and attitudes are under scrutiny.

However, we often find that measuring people can have a negative effect, in contrast to the positive effect seen during the lighting level studies. People may resent being monitored in this way, especially if they suspect that the organization does not have their best interests at heart, and start muttering about 'thought police' and infringement of personal privacy. I was once involved with a visit by a group of influential overseas customers who had strict religious views on certain subjects; consequently, one of our managers asked the female staff to dress demurely for the duration of the visit and carried out an informal 'measurement' by wandering around and to check how the women were dressed each day. Everybody resented the request far less than the monitoring; although they complied, their eagerness to please the customers decreased, they made representations to discover whether anybody had ever previously complained that the female staff in the office had dressed inappropriately for work and they became, for a while, less tolerant of further requests from the same manager.

There are three lessons here. The first is that we must understand that any measurement or monitoring of people will have an effect on them and we should try to plan how we introduce and design those measurements to minimize any negative impacts and enhance the positive ones. The second is that effects may not necessarily surface directly in the area being measured – for example, measuring punctuality may have a positive effect on timekeeping but could mean that less time is spent on productive work when actually present. (This arises from natural contrariness – 'The company may well insist that I am here early, but I'll have my morning cup of tea at work now instead of at home'.) The third is that, in certain cases, the negative effects will be there no matter how good our intentions are; all we can do is to work to reduce them on the understanding that we can never fully eliminate them.

MEASUREMENT CRITERIA

So far, we have explored a number of ways in which a list of measurements can be identified. Ideally, the list should be generated from at least two different sources to ensure that we have a balanced and meaningful set. For instance, we could have one list created by a dedicated measurement team and another created from topics considered as important by the organization's leaders. However, this exercise is unlikely to definitely answer the question of what people characteristics we should measure. We should treat the resultant list as a starting point, rather like the ideas generated from a brainstorming exercise. From there we need to apply some form of criteria to filter the list down to something more meaningful and useful.

The measurements that we choose must be:

- *Quantifiable.* It should be possible to apply a numeric value to what we measure on some form of scale. This is particularly difficult for a significant proportion of people measurements, since many factors are rather subjective, but it must be theoretically possible to define a numeric scale (more on this topic in subsequent chapters). Although 'is it or isn't it?' is often defined as quantifiable – that is, the value can be 1 or 0 – this represents a rather flimsy numeric scale. For measurements to be really useful it is not enough to choose something that is on or off – did they or didn't they? – since this is too polarized to be of much use in subsequent analysis.

- *Understandable.* It should be possible for people who are being measured (since we really will alienate them if we not only study them but then keep the results secret) and the people using the measurements to easily understand what the data represents, what it means and what changes mean. This means that, although complicated indices calculated in a formula from multiple inputs may sometimes be necessary, they need to be used with caution.

- *Acceptable.* The people being measured must accept that the way in which the data are collected, interpreted, analysed and used is 'fair' and reasonable. For example, they may not appreciate and accept counting the number of toilet breaks that an individual takes in a day since our physiological needs are all different and there may be embarrassing, personal reasons why our patterns temporarily change.

- *Representative.* What is being monitored must actually represent what it is intended to represent. Politicians, for example, often choose not to apply this rule, often being accused of quoting statistics that reinforce the point they wish to make rather than truly reflecting the actual state of affairs. If people feel that measurement results are being manipulated, or have some form of 'spin' put on them, they will never accept their validity.

- *Available.* Measurements are useless if they are not up-to-date. One of the biggest pitfalls of a measurement programme is to publish the results some considerable time after the measurement was actually taken. The results of measurements must be available immediately (that is, within a sensible timeframe for the nature of the specific measurement), and must always be current.

- *Sensitive.* Whatever measurement or index is selected, it must reflect changes in the underlying situation. For example, there is little point in using the number of telephone calls answered in a day to judge the telephonist's current level of enthusiasm; unless the situation has become so extreme that calls are left to ring unanswered, the number of calls actually dealt with will largely correlate to how many calls are actually made to the organization and will not alter if the telephonist's enthusiasm wanes.

- *Stable.* Similarly, the measurement must show steady results for steady performance; if somebody behaves and feels the same way today as yesterday then our measurement should produce the same result. If too many external factors affect the measurement, it is of little value.

Any measurement that we design that fails to meet these tests should be questioned. Will it really add any value to what we are trying to achieve?

SUMMARY

- Choosing what to measure about people is less obvious than choosing product or process measurements.
- The list has to come from careful thought about what people do and feel, rather than by process analysis.
- Measurements should reflect what people want, as well as what is wanted of them.
- We need to beware of just measuring what we are able to measure, rather than trying to identify what we should measure.
- Measurements can be defined as describing behaviours (what people do) or beliefs (what people think).
- Beliefs are harder to measure than behaviours and may have less value.
- Some behaviours are closely linked; linked factors should all be measured to achieve a full picture.
- Understanding what we mean by a behaviour often requires us to 'drill down' to understand the hierarchies involved.
- There may be links between measurements of people and those looking at processes or customer satisfaction, but there are likely to be few links with traditional financial measurements.
- People measurements can address most areas of the measurement continuum, although they tend more towards the strategic end since they represent longer-term factors than do many process measurements.
- The fact that measuring people will itself have an effect on their behaviour has to be allowed for.
- Good measurements should be relevant, sensitive to change, constant in stability and broadly accepted for them to be workable.

CHAPTER FIVE

Human Measurement Techniques

THE UNCERTAINTY OF MEASURING PEOPLE

When we measure in any traditional way, we are fairly certain of the results. If we want to find out the size of our window frame in order to have curtains made we know that what the ruler or tape reveals is correct. If we measure the temperature of a furnace there are ways of making sure that the gauge is giving the right reading.

When measuring factors associated with people, though, it is clear that things are very different. Deciding just how enthusiastic somebody is does not lend itself to international units of measure or precise calibration of data collection techniques. Even knowing whether a certain behaviour or action represents something positive or negative can be open to question; two managers asked to provide career development activities for an individual may take different paths, one setting up a detailed training and experience plan with close supervision and support while the other attempts to achieve the same aim through allowing the employee a high degree of freedom and autonomy. So we may not even be able to have a definitive view of what should be measured or what the signs mean, let alone have the luxuries available to engineers of standard scales or calibrated equipment.

This problem need not be insurmountable, as long as we understand that the uncertainty exists and prepare to deal with it. Even engineers and scientists, whose job it is to use verifiable mathematics to support their theories and projects, recognize the existence of measurement uncertainty. Physicists were taught by Heisenberg that the more closely one attempts to pin down the movements of atomic particles the less certain they can be about what is actually happening. Even closer to home for those involved in managing an organization, technical process measurements are accepted to have a level of uncertainty owing to the inherent variability and inaccuracy of the test equipment used and the influence of human beings on the measurements taken. In the last case, engineers try to define the level of uncertainty in a particular measurement by identifying all the possible sources of error and how large they could be, then creating a prediction of the total possible error via a simple sum; the resultant figure is then known as the measurement uncertainty.

We can use a similar approach when dealing with people measurements. When we quote the results of our analyses, anybody with any intelligence will realize that there is a margin of error in our data. We can anticipate this and increase the level of acceptance of our results by identifying in advance where we think there is a possible source of error and how large that error might be. Having identified the enemy, so to speak, we can then take steps to minimize the impact of any uncertainties:

- Choose as large a sample size as possible for the measurement; this will tend to reduce the effect of any one measurement being erroneous.
- Make more than one measurement of each person, thereby reducing the effect of any one measurement.
- Use more than one method of taking the measurements and/or collecting the data (which could involve, for example, two different people making independent judgements on the prevailing conditions).

● Define close rules on how a behaviour or other measured element should be evaluated, making it more likely that the same evaluation criteria are applied each time.
● Keep the measurement programme focused on clearly targeted objectives.

These steps will never bring the measurement of people to the level of precision that is found, for example, when a quality control inspector determines the diameter of a spindle, but once the problem of uncertainty is understood it can be managed and catered for. Such barriers and pitfalls, once conceived, are relatively straightforward to deal with, although we will explore some of them at various points later in the book, especially the use of rules on how to quantify behaviours.

GAINING OBJECTIVITY

When trying to measure people we need to obtain the right balance between intuition and science. I have already emphasized the need to use one's feelings and intuition to judge the circumstances that we are investigating. This is essential: if we fail to do this, we may miss vital factors that do not crop up as part of standard measurements or might allow a badly designed measurement programme to lead us astray. It is this last point that I always consider to be so important when looking at any data; perhaps one of the biggest errors that my daughters ever make during their mathematics homework is to perform a calculation quickly and not check the result for sense. As a result, their sums sometimes prove that an elephant weighs a few kilograms instead of a few tons, or that the average walking pace is 60 km/h. If they simply thought about whether the answers were sensible they would make far fewer errors.

This philosophy is just as useful when measuring people. It is entirely possible that the way in which we evaluate what people are doing presents us with results that are completely surprising. There could be two reasons for this: that we were not as in touch with the employees as we thought we were or that there is something wrong with the measurement. If the results are not what we would have expected, then we need to look at the picture again; we will have to check the data and analyses to ensure that we have not made an error.

Ideally, though, we should have designed the measurement regime to be objective enough to guarantee that the results will be accurate (or as good as they can be when there are large uncertainties). This requires a system that defines rules and guidelines for each and every measurement, so that data is based on some sort of objective evaluation criteria rather than on whim or prejudice. For example, when filling in questionnaires (especially those that have no direct importance to me) I tend to make an overall judgement about what I am being asked about and mark every answer at that level, except for a few items on the list where I vary it up or down a little at random to make it less boring; it is just such whimsical data that we must try to avoid.

Objectivity is not only important for making sure that measurements are accurate, it is also an essential component for ensuring short- and long-term viability, as will be explored in later chapters.

USING EVALUATION CRITERIA

SETTING THE SCALE

One of the first steps in designing a measurement is to define the scale. We are all used to this and it is an obvious thing to do; schools use percentage scores for examinations and often employ a letter scale – 'A, B, C, D, E' – for other work. Thermometers use the predetermined standard scales of Celsius (centigrade) or Fahrenheit. Customer satisfaction surveys typically have five or six choices ranging from 'perfectly satisfied' to 'completely dissatisfied' or similar.

Table 5.1 Quantifying the measurement scale

Survey option	Score
Perfectly satisfied	6
Satisfied	5
Reasonably satisfied	4
Slightly dissatisfied	3
Very dissatisfied	2
Completely dissatisfied	1

When designing a scale for our own people measurement programme it is best to choose a scale that is both numerical and qualitative. So, for example, we could have the satisfaction survey options mentioned in the paragraph above, but we should also assign a numerical value to each so that the data is quantifiable. Thus if there are six options then we should assign a 'score' of one to six for them. We then end up with something resembling Table 5.1.

The description of each step in the scale allows us to perform subsequent analysis, draw charts and so on, and the description allows the person being measured to see what each step means. This last point is especially important in surveys.

There are a number of guidelines for setting the scale:

- Make it large enough to provide a good range (only two options is usually insufficient) but not so large that the difference between one step and the next is meaningless (if I am presented with a scale of 1 to 100 for my satisfaction with your service, I am unlikely to think too hard about whether to mark it as 70 or 71 and, in fact, will probably readjust the scale myself into smaller steps by only allocating scores in steps of five, for example).
- It is often a good idea to choose an even number of options to prevent people from appearing completely neutral. Again, this is very important in surveys where the person is marking their own score.
- Zero can be used in the scale but only with caution, since it does tend to skew the results (there is a far greater difference between 0 and 1 than there is between 1 and 2). I tend to use zeroes only to indicate that the item is not applicable to that person then set my spreadsheet to ignore any zeroes, rather than include them in the total.
- There should be even steps between the points on the scale, otherwise analysis is extremely difficult. This might seem obvious, but it does also mean that the description of each point has to be chosen carefully; if the descriptions of two neighbouring points on the scale seem to indicate a much wider or narrower gap than between other points it could lead to incorrect measurement.

DEFINING CRITERIA FOR THE SCALE

Once we have the scale defined, as well as a numerical value and a description assigned to each step, it is tempting to proceed with collecting the data, allocating a value to each person's opinion/behaviour/attributes according to the judgement of the person making the measurement. However, this is not really sufficiently objective; just because each possible choice carries a description does not mean that people will find it easy to make the right choice. For example, many end-of-event training course evaluation sheets have 'excellent' as the top of the scale. My own definition of excellence is that it is so good that it is difficult to see how any improvement could be made, which means that true excellence is hardly ever found. Others, though, seem happy to rate a course as excellent if they have enjoyed it and learnt something.

What is needed is something to increase the objectivity and repeatability of the measurements, so that two people measuring the same experience or person are more likely to produce the same result.

A good way of doing this is to set precise criteria for each point on the measurement scale – in other words, to state exactly what is intended by each of the descriptions. This gives the evaluator clear guidelines on exactly where to position the measurement, depending on the circumstances observed or experienced.

To illustrate this, I have taken the satisfaction example shown in Table 5.1 and added an extra column that defines the criteria, as shown in Table 5.2.

Table 5.2   Measurement scale criteria

Survey option	Score	Criteria
Perfectly satisfied	6	All my training objectives have been met; my individual needs were considered within course constraints; the syllabus was fully covered; appropriate new skills/knowledge have been gathered; the trainer was competent; the timetable was adhered to; no complaints about facilities or refreshments.
Satisfied	5	At the least the most important of my training objectives have been met; the syllabus was adhered to; some new skills/knowledge have been gathered; competent trainer; timetable generally adhered to.
Reasonably satisfied	4	Some of my training objectives have been met; some new skills/knowledge have been acquired or existing ones reinforced; acceptable trainer.
Slightly dissatisfied	3	Some of my training objectives have been met; some new skills/knowledge have been acquired or existing ones reinforced; acceptable trainer; some improvements to syllabus, timetabling, timekeeping and/or facilities required.
Very dissatisfied	2	Few of my training objectives have been met; little or no new skills/knowledge have been acquired; significant improvements needed to trainer competence, syllabus, timetabling and so on.
Completely dissatisfied	1	The nature of the course syllabus and its delivery were totally inappropriate to my needs.

This is a simple example adapted from some guidelines given by a training company to those filling in the 'happy sheet' (a name often used for the participant satisfaction form traditionally given out at the end of the course). Note the way in which the guidelines are described: they attempt to clearly steer the allocated score towards particular levels depending on what the training course participants experienced. For instance, if they were reasonably pleased with the training material itself and the way in which the trainer presented it, but really hated the food and the sleeping arrangements, the worst score that they can give is a 3, representing 'slightly dissatisfied' since lower scores require the training itself to be of poor quality. Similarly, participants who have not really benefited from the course but really enjoyed the time away from work and had a marvellous time using the pool, gymnasium and nightclub in the course hotel are discouraged from giving high scores since the form encourages the participants to allocate scores on the most important things that affect the quality of the training and allows less room for adjustment based on peripheral elements of the training experience.

In fact, most training companies do not use such guidelines for their participants because trainers know that if they do something that is fun and interesting right at the end of the course, just before the 'happy sheets' are given out, the trainees will feel good and will award higher scores. This makes the trainer look better in the eyes of their employer and also helps the training company refute any subsequent claims or complaints from the participant's employer. This merely reinforces my point: everyone knows that these end-of-course satisfaction sheets do not really reflect how good the training was, and in fact they are treated as something of a joke in some quarters. Using precise definitions of each score would alleviate this problem and make the measurements more reliable.

TECHNIQUES OF MEASUREMENT

A number of different techniques can be used to obtain measurements of the actual and potential contributions of our people. These vary from basic questionnaires in which a person expresses their own viewpoint, such as in the training course response sheet mentioned above, to forms of data gathering where an independent person attempts to make the evaluation by reading of particular signs and indicators, just as a technician judges the state of a machine by reading the appropriate dials and gauges.

These techniques fall into three basic categories: self-assessment, second-party assessment (that is, assessment by others) and sign reading.

SELF-ASSESSMENT

Self-assessment involves asking an individual (or sometimes a group) to identify their own attitudes and behaviours, and is typified by the questionnaire. We are all familiar with the satisfaction questionnaire that increasing numbers of businesses ask us to complete these days. We are given them (as already mentioned) at training courses, in hotels and restaurants, when we have our cars serviced and even on the Monday morning when the gas man comes to call.

These are all forms of customer satisfaction survey, which is the most common type of self-measurement. Such surveys attempt to gather information from customers on how well our organization is serving their needs by asking them to complete a simple checklist and send it back to an appropriate person in the organization for analysis. The results are used both to identify problems that individual customers have experienced and to make some overall judgement of how well we are performing.

They achieve the second of these aims better than the first. The end-of-course questionnaire described earlier falls into this category and is a good example of how it works. If I run a course for 12 people, they all complete the form and are pleased with all the aspects about which questions are asked, except for one individual who gives low scores for the same elements, what am I to think? Everyone else was satisfied, so why is just one person displeased? The easy reaction, under such circumstances, is to decide that one cannot please all the people all of the time so the complainer, being in a minority, must just have been having a bad day and decided to take it out on me. Similarly, if a hotel changes its front desk arrangement and most people compliment the new level of service that it brings but one guest hates it, we tend to assume that we have made a change that is generally welcomed by customers and will take no account of the lone voice.

Self-assessment questionnaires range from a single-sided slip of paper, such as might be found on a restaurant table, to detailed documents several pages long, such as companies might give to major customers with whom they hope to develop longstanding relationships. They all, however, represent the same basic approach, with standard questions given to every respondent and a predetermined set of possible answers to each one.

Note that there are some customer satisfaction questionnaires that do not use multiple-choice questions but ask those filling in the form to give their answers in words (for example, 'With which aspect of your stay in our hotel have you been most pleased?'). These require much more work to evaluate. They are valid forms of survey, but do not really represent true measurements since it is not possible to quantify and analyse the resultant data in the same manner as we are considering in this book.

These days, electronic versions, such as online questionnaires on the Internet, are becoming increasingly popular. They are essentially the same thing, although they do represent a greater opportunity to be more innovative in terms of design – for example, basing the choice of which question to present next on previous answers (paper versions can achieve this in a basic fashion by asking a respondent to jump to a later question if they answer 'No' to this one, but give less opportunity for direct tailoring to responses).

Although customer satisfaction questionnaires are the most common of this form of measurement, they are also found in other guises. One, in particular, that may be familiar is the employee survey which seeks to identify how people in the organization feel and think from a standard set of questions that they are asked to complete and return to a central point. This type of self-assessment measurement is one way of achieving exactly what we are discussing in this book and we will explore its use in Chapter Six. Indeed, many managers, when asked to measure their people, leap immediately to the conclusion that they need to run an employee survey. As we will see below, there are other ways of doing it, but the employee survey is certainly the most obvious and the most frequently employed – and is a perfectly valid tool.

SECOND-PARTY ASSESSMENT

Second-party assessment involves asking one person to determine the attributes of another. The third category of people measurement, using continuous monitoring, discussed below also uses one person (or a group of persons) to evaluate others but there is a key difference: second-party assessment assumes that the person being measured is directly conscious of the measurement process, whereas the continuous monitoring does not.

Just as self-assessment finds its most common form in the questionnaire, so second-party assessment is most frequently embodied in the interview. This involves some suitably trained and experienced expert discussing one or more topics with someone (usually one-to-one, but it can be with a group) and using their insight and knowledge to interpret the answers.

Readers may make the connection here with the type of interview that is often conducted by market research personnel; a number of questions are asked and the interviewee is asked to choose the best answer from a list. This, in fact, is simply an extension of the self-assessment process – a facilitated self-assessment questionnaire. The interviewers take standard questions and standard responses and simply check the appropriate item on their sheet in response to what the interviewee says. Their input to the measurement process is:

- to encourage the interviewee to answer the questions quickly (that is, immediately) and fully
- to help clarify what the questions mean
- to provide guidance on the specific interpretation of each possible answer (replacing the written version that I discussed under 'using evaluation criteria' earlier in this chapter, which may be tedious and time-consuming for the person to read).

Although this technique has some validity – for example, the results tend to be more accurate than those from a survey where the respondent is left to answer the questions on their own – it is, in fact, simply an extension of the survey by questionnaire method. What we will consider here is another method of interview which does require answers to specific questions (since without being specific we cannot really measure) but does not just involve asking direct questions and writing down the answers verbatim as selected from a list. It involves discussing the topics of interest generally with one or more people and drawing conclusions from the interview as a whole.

The second-party assessment requires the use of a trained and experienced interviewer who can pick out the nuances from an interview and interpret the results appropriately. It is often used to replace or reinforce self-assessment where it is suspected that answers to questionnaires may not be representative of the true picture, perhaps because people are frightened to reveal what they truly think or because only those who wish to complain bother to complete the questionnaires assiduously. It does, however, have some potential disadvantages:

- The presence of the interviewer might intimidate those being measured.
- The interviewer's own interpretations can colour the results.
- It is much more time-consuming than the simple survey.

We will discuss ways of conducting and managing such a measurement approach in Chapter Seven.

SIGNS

The third category is the indirect, or continuous monitoring, method of measuring people. This involves looking for events and indicators that can be used to build up a picture of what is going on. It avoids directly asking people for the answers to the measurement or related questions, either through questionnaire or interview, but looks for those things that can be observed and quantified on which to base an analysis.

This type of measurement has certain advantages over the previous two:

- It can measure aspects of people that are hard to pin down simply through asking questions.
- It is much less obtrusive (and can even be done without the direct knowledge of those being measured, if desired).
- It may be more acceptable in the workplace than the previous two methods, both of which require the person to take time away from their work.
- It is far more versatile in that its output can be immediate, typically requiring less analysis than the first two categories.

Looking for signs does have a drawback in that it is more difficult to define and establish than, for example, simply obtaining a questionnaire and asking everybody to fill it in. It is, however, my favourite method since it lends itself best to continuity and a professional measurement approach. It also equates more closely to the types of process measurement that are conducted elsewhere in the organization and thus represents a better fit with other management tools. Using signs-based measurement also allows us best to adopt the rules and guidelines which I have already discussed and which make up a successful approach to evaluating the feelings and behaviours of people. We will explore this topic in more detail in Chapter Eight.

OBJECTIVES AND RESULTS

An integral part of the measurement programme must be setting objectives. These will arise either because the measurements themselves show that we need some change in a particular area or because we already know that there are problems and measurement is one of the tools that we wish to use to help tackle them.

The objectives for change must be seen as being overall company aims and not those of the measurement programme. It is important to remember that measurement cannot bring about change, any more than a pressure gauge can top up our depleted petrol tank; it merely indicates that some further action is necessary. Measurement of people is the same; it shows us where to focus our attentions but does not make the change.

This is an especially important point for executives who are commissioning a people measurement programme. If they simply set up such a scheme and hope that their problems will automatically be resolved then they have completely misunderstood what measurement is all about. They will still need to design and operate a change programme which targets and achieves appropriate objectives. The measurements will only help them choose which areas in which to set improvement objectives and find out how well those improvements are progressing. It is particularly important that this is clearly made part of the 'contract' between executives and the person in charge of the measurement programme; they should be judged on how well the workforce is measured and not on how well they perform ('don't shoot the messenger' comes to mind here) – unless, of course, the person in charge of measurement is also the person running the improvement programme.

DIRECT AND INDIRECT INDICATORS

UNDERSTANDING THE DIFFERENCE

There are some things that we can measure directly and others that can only be derived from analysing a number of indicators and drawing suitable conclusions. It is important to recognize this when drawing up our system. We must be aware of which are direct and which are indirect indicators and treat them accordingly.

DIRECT INDICATORS

Direct indicators tell us what we need to know in a straightforward manner. For example, if we are interested in the punctuality of our workforce then monitoring their arrival times will represent a direct measurement. It may not tell us the whole picture; we may also wish to monitor the time taken for breaks and departure time to gain a complete view, but each of these directly indicates the aspect under consideration. Thus, a direct indicator does not need to be the only factor used, but it should not require any translation to tell us what we need to know. Other examples of direct indicators are:

- work rate, measured as the number of fault-free tasks dealt with (units made, orders processed, calls handled and so on) in a period of time
- the number of times that an employee has to be spoken to about breaking rules as a direct indicator of their compliance with company policies (or at least, their detected rate of compliance)
- questionnaire results relating to specific issues, such as the end-of-course critiques that directly indicate the customer's perception of the trainer's abilities.

INDIRECT INDICATORS

Indirect indicators are employed where it is not possible to measure what we are seeking directly, or perhaps where readily available data is considered useful but has to be interpreted before it can relate to a factor of interest. The medical profession is very familiar with this concept; a patient does not come to a doctor with the name of their illness stamped on their forehead but instead they have to understand all the signs and symptoms (each of which on their own could mean a number of different things) and make a diagnosis by putting all the data together.

One of the best known examples of the use of indirect indicators for individual personal measurement is the reading of body language. Many of us may have heard about small signs are meant to indicate something larger – for example, when a woman crosses her legs towards a man she is displaying sexual interest, or if someone touches their nose when speaking it means that they are not telling the truth. Most intelligent people will realize that this is completely ridiculous. If I rub my nose, it is most likely because it itches and the bit about leg-crossing is probably just wishful thinking on the part of many men. Nevertheless, these signs do have some validity. Body language works in clusters; if I see one sign on its own it is probably meaningless, but if I see six or seven close together, all of which indicate the same thing, then there is a strong probability (although still not a certainty) that the signs can be interpreted in a certain way.

This is exactly how any indirect indicators should be treated. The strength or weakness of one indicator is not enough, on its own, for us to draw a conclusion. Several of them, however, all moving in the same direction make it reasonable for us to assume that we are witnessing a particular form of behaviour or feeling. Other examples of indirect indicators are:

- yawning, stretching and fidgeting as signs of tiredness or irritation
- large numbers of messages (e-mails, memos and so on) on trivial topics that may show a lack of enthusiasm for the main task
- talking that stops when the boss enters the room, possibly indicating lack of attention to the work in hand (although it may not – they might just have been talking about how to resolve a tricky situation without having to get the boss involved)
- an increasing backlog of work as an indicator of a number of underlying problems such as poor management and leadership, ineffective processes, low motivation, underresourcing and so on.

One cautionary tale: I mentioned above that doctors regularly use indirect indicators but even they can get it wrong if they do not take the time and trouble to perform an adequate analysis. At the age of 33 I visited my GP and, when asked what was wrong with me, I simply pointed to my very red and spotty face. 'Ah yes,' pronounced the doctor, 'your acne's become a bit angry. I'll give you some cream.' It was only after reminding the doctor that I was beyond adolescence and that he had recently treated my daughter for an illness that he agreed with my own suspicions that I was suffering from chickenpox (although I accept that this is probably just as rare in an adult as severe acne). One must be very careful about jumping to hasty conclusions when using indirect indicators.

QUANTIFICATION

We have already discussed the need to allocate a scale to what we are measuring and to allocate a numerical value to each point on the scale. One further point to consider is that we have the opportunity, if we wish, to make the scale against which we take the measurements different to that by which we conduct the analysis. To explain what I mean it is easiest to look at an example. Consider the simple table of measurements shown in Table 5.3. These measurements were taken using a scale of 1 to 5. If we restrict ourselves to using the same scale for publishing the overall results, then we are limited to reporting the modal average (that is, the value that is most often found) which in this case is 4. To report the findings as 4, however, would be misleading since this, as well as being the most often

Table 5.3   Example measurements on a simple scale

Person	Score
Employee 1	4
Employee 2	4
Employee 3	3
Employee 4	2
Employee 5	4
Employee 6	2
Employee 7	4
Employee 8	1
Employee 9	1
Employee 10	4

reported measurement, is also the highest. In this case, we need to either allow smaller increments in our analysis scale – tenths or hundredths of a unit, perhaps – or maybe even recalculate the scale in another way, such as using a percentage value, making 1 worth 10 per cent, 2 worth 20 per cent and so on. The we can take the mean average (the total divided by the sample size) which gives us a value of 3.5 or 70 per cent, much more representative of what actually was reported. When conducting our analysis and publishing our results, we nearly always need to use a finer scale than we used when taking the actual measurements.

PITFALLS

FOREWARNED IS FOREARMED

There are a number of things that can obstruct a good measurement programme, as well as traps into which the unwary can fall. Knowing what they are is half the battle in overcoming them. A few of them are discussed below.

MEASURING 'PAST THE POST'

This is probably the most common error when taking business measurements of any kind. For some reason, and it seems quite inexplicable to me, many of those given the responsibility for measurement seem to opt for measuring how much of the data is above or below a certain threshold, rather than quantifying the data itself.

To illustrate the point and for continuity, let us look again at the example of a training course satisfaction questionnaire. Such a questionnaire may well have five options in each category, to which we will allocate a score of 1 to 5. Many organizations, quite rightly, set targets for such measurements and may well have an internal policy that a score of better than 3 is desired. This leads to the temptation to simply count the percentage of marks that are above 3 and use that as the measurement.

However, this only gives an indirect measurement; if we discover that 70 per cent of results are above 3 it only gives us limited information. How bad, for example, were the 30 per cent of scores that were at 3 or below? We gain far more information about the pattern of student feedback if we analyse the data directly, producing graphs and overall scores based on the raw data rather than the data compared to a benchmark. What we should do is just report the mean and range of the scores given, not the exceptions to a rule or target.

There is nothing wrong in having a target, of course (bearing in mind that people measurements have a degree of subjectivity and uncertainty so that targets have to be treated with caution). We can envisage a graph of the data as shown in Figure 5.1, where the target level is drawn on the graph to indicate where we meet the target and where we do not. This gives us a much better picture of what is going on. We can immediately see where our target has been met and where it has not, without having to perform a secondary calculation against the target value. It also has great strength if we ever decide to alter our target level; all we need to do is move the line on our graph and we can see both how new and old data fit the new requirement. If, on the other hand, we use a technique that counts the number of instances above or below a certain value then changing the target level will require us to completely recalculate all historical data in order to see how well we performed.

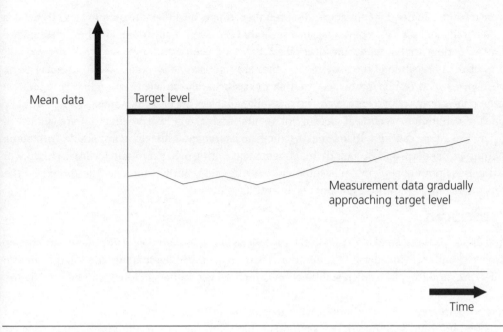

Figure 5.1   Target indication

This is not to say that using 'past the post' techniques is never appropriate. If there is a definite limit that represents a specification or pass mark, then obviously it is important to know how many instances fail to meet the criteria – a school, for example, wish to know how many pupils passed and failed an examination and a manufacturer would wish to know how many defective items it has made. Yet this is only part of the picture, since we also need to know, for instance, how badly pupils failed – did they just miss the target or were their grades disastrous? In almost every case, if we have defined suitable quantified scales for our measurement, it is always better to measure performance against that scale directly; if we are measuring how many pass the post, this should be in addition to, not instead of, direct measurement.

TAKING NUMBERS TOO SERIOUSLY

Remember: there are lies, damn lies and statistics. Although we are trying to create a measurement system that is objective and repeatable, there will inevitably be ways in which we can manipulate the data to make it look different, depending on our objectives. A common example of this is the pitfall mentioned above of measuring past the post instead of directly, which can drastically alter the way the data look (for example, if a food manufacturer measures the number of jars that contain below the minimum weight of product, this might hide the fact that they are all being overfilled thereby wasting money and causing sealing difficulties). Such an effect is exacerbated when we are measuring people since these types of measurement are subject to greater uncertainty than others. Measuring the weight of product in a jar holds far greater inherent clarity than does measuring how cheerful our staff sound on the telephone.

We must remember, therefore, not to treat the data produced from a measurement exercise too precisely. Just because our result last month was 3.75 and this month it is 3.9 does not necessarily mean that we have had a 4 per cent increase. In fact, depending on the nature of what we are looking at, it may mean that we don't have an increase at all. Only a sustained movement will indicate whether things are changing in the right direction, and even then, it may be difficult to quantify exactly what is going on. For instance, we may have chosen a scale that is only partially used; if we have defined the top score as 'perfect' then nobody may ever select that option since nothing is ever truly perfect, and they may also ignore some of the lower scores that are represented as being so bad as never to be sensible choices. This results in only a portion of the scale being actually used, so that comparative measurements is terms of percentage growth or similar analyses are fairly meaningless since we have no means of calibration. Technical measurements are made using instruments that are subject to specific routines that calibrate them, making their measurements directly comparable with some predetermined standard, and we cannot do this when measuring behaviours and feelings. This lack of calibration does not make people measurements meaningless, but we must bear in mind that the numbers produced are indicators and not necessarily absolute values.

HASTY DECISIONS

A related danger is that of making excessively quick decisions based on the results of measurements. Because we cannot provide absolute calibration of our data, any individual measurement is of little use on its own, and therefore any result must be compared with others before it can be used in any way.

Even with this knowledge, though, we can still be tempted to be overhasty in our use of measurement information. An initial measurement that is low may not prompt us to action because we do not have a benchmark against which to judge it, but it could encourage us to consider a second measurement showing an even lower value as an indication of worsening performance requiring corrective action. In fact, it is much better to wait until far more data are available and a trend is confirmed before jumping into action. As discussed above, a small apparent change could, in fact, be due to normal uncertainty rather than a real trend or change. Exercising patience is far more likely to result in a firmer foundation for any decisions than would any form of hastiness.

MEASURING BECAUSE WE CAN

Measurements should be chosen by identifying the principal categories in which we are interested and looking at our objectives and ambitions. This is the most logical and likely approach to be taken by anyone who plans their measurement programme carefully. However, despite the best will in the world, it is easy to fall into the trap of choosing to take a measurement just because we can. Even the best of us might narrow down what we are looking at to a certain point and then stumble across something that we can measure and seize upon it. Just because it initially seems to be useful and the data are accessible, however, does not mean that we really want to measure it.

My favourite real-life example of this is a projects company that was implementing a total quality management (TQM) programme and determined that they must measure their quality performance. They decided, sensibly, that they would only choose a few measurements to begin with and work up to a more comprehensive set once they gained sufficient experience. They duly created a set of three measurements that they believed to measure quality. These were:

● numbers of customer complaints
● the numbers of repeat service visits (that is, occasions when a technician had to be sent back to a job because the original visit had not solved the problem)
● the difference between costs actually incurred in a project and those estimated at the quotation stage.

The first of these is a traditional quality measure in all businesses and the second is quite common in the service industry. The third is something that the company felt strongly about; if they made significant errors in the estimation of project costs, their profitability could be sorely affected. It was also not difficult to make the measurement since the input and output data were both available; they had simply not been put together before. It was a valid and useful measurement. The mistake, however, was that the measurement does not represent 'quality', mainly because it has no direct impact on the customer (as long as the customer gets the promised service at the agreed price, they do not really care about what goes on internally at their supplier). The measurement was aimed at the internal efficacy of the quotation process; it therefore represented something of great interest to some managers but was not in keeping with the primary objective of the measurement programme. Now, it is possible that what the company's management really wanted was a system of measuring key elements of their business performance and 'quality' was just a handle on which to hang the concept. Either way, though, the idea had not been thought through sufficiently to ensure that the measurements being taken fitted the agreed strategy and objectives.

This type of example is not uncommon. The easiest measurements to make are usually those concerned with money, since they are already expressed in numerical terms. It may be useful for the organization to monitor such measurements, it is also likely that many of them will have little to do with measuring people, and we should not aim to squeeze them into our people monitoring programme just because they represent data that is readily available.

TOO NARROW A SELF-INTEREST

To be truly objective also requires allowing room for some discomfort. As I have already pointed out, we may already have some idea of what people measurements might tell us. There is nothing wrong with this as long as it does not lead us into prejudging the issues.

There is a danger that we may shy away from those topics that we suspect may give us 'undesirable' information. If the person or team running the measurement programme suspects that there is an area that might show them in a bad light, they may simply choose not to measure it. To avoid this we need, of course, a degree of professionalism amongst our leaders. It is also helpful to remember the purpose of a measurement programme; it is not there to enable us to lay blame and criticize, but to highlight where action is required. Thus our first reaction when seeing a measurement with poorer outcomes than we would like should be 'That's interesting. It looks as if we need to do some work in that area' and not to find somebody to shout at.

We must also ensure that the people being measured do not see the programme as a means for them to make personal gains. The results of measurements should not be used to satisfy individual grievances, for which there should already be a process in place. People should not be led to believe that measurements will automatically lead to better pay and conditions if they use an employee survey, for example, as an opportunity to grumble.

Similarly, those involved in running the measurements ought not to be given the opportunity to use it for their personal objectives; we all know that some questions and ideas can be phrased in such a way that significantly swings the likely responses in one direction or another, and some may be tempted to try to manipulate measurements in their own self-interest. For this reason I suggest that the best approach is to establish a measurement committee to oversee any people measurement programme (setting up and running such a committee is discussed later in the book).

Finally, the organization itself must not take self-interest too far when measuring people. Although the primary purpose must be to improve the overall way in which the business runs, it must be done in an enlightened fashion, so that it is clearly understood that welfare and motivation of people will ultimately lead to a successful operation.

SUMMARY

- There is uncertainty involved in measuring people – single data sets rarely represent anything absolute.
- Understanding this uncertainty is key to using measurements well.
- Being as objective as possible will keep the level of uncertainty to a minimum.
- For each measurement, we should set a scale that is individually selected to gain maximum information.
- The meaning of each point on the scale should be defined to improve the accuracy of measurements and analysis.
- There are three basic people measurement techniques: a questionnaire completed by people themselves, an interview programme, and continuous monitoring by looking for signs.
- Setting aims and objectives will help us know what we are measuring, why we are measuring it and what results we are hoping for.
- Some measurements will tell us exactly what we are looking for – for example, measuring attendance hours directly tells us about attendance levels.
- Some measurements are indirect, which means that a change in their value points to a change in something else that we are really interested in but which is hard to measure directly.
- Often the scale that we use to report measurements may be more detailed than the original scale used to collect the data.
- There are a number of pitfalls to be avoided; these should be considered in advance so that the programme can be designed to avoid them.
- A key danger is measuring the number of exceptions rather than the data itself; this drastically reduces the value of the information.
- Because measuring people is not a precise science, we must not take the numerical results resulting from our analyses as hard and fast values.
- For the same reason, teams should not rush into action on the basis of a single set of results.
- Measurements should be chosen to fit our aims and objectives, not measured simply because the data is easily available.
- Self-interest amongst managers and measurement teams can influence what is measured and how the results are interpreted; this is a stronger danger than in many operational measurement programmes since personal issues are directly involved.

CHAPTER SIX

Employee Surveys

THE USE OF EMPLOYEE SURVEYS

The employee survey is the most obvious and most common way of measuring the opinions and attitudes of people within any organization. It usually relies on a form of questionnaire with a large number of questions, possibly grouped under a number of different topics. This is then completed by the individuals being surveyed, and the results are subsequently analysed and acted upon by, or on behalf of, the leaders of the organization.

Many large companies make the employee survey a regular event. This has a number of advantages over the one-off approach:

- It enables comparisons to be made over a period of time – remember that measurements of people are not absolute and so are only really meaningful via comparison.
- It allows some calibration of the measurements – for example, we can include some aspects in the survey to which we know the answer and find out what 'score' is obtained in that area, or can compare scores in known good times against those resulting from a survey in bad times.
- It sends the message to the people being surveyed that their views are continually welcomed and that the survey is not just a fad.

Nevertheless, there are some problems associated with running such surveys frequently. The first of these is that a full survey represents a great deal of work in preparation, implementation, analysis and reporting and the more frequently it is conducted the more work there is. The second is that the exercise can become stale. If an individual receives the same questionnaire three times and they feel that they have little different to say since last time, they will not be highly motivated to give it the attention it deserves. On the other hand, if the design of the questionnaire changes radically from one instance to the next, it will be impossible to meaningfully compare results.

A good survey is run regularly enough to keep people measurement active without becoming too great an administrative burden. It should maintain some consistency between one session and the next, while being flexible enough to allow for changes in circumstances and previous results. There should be a balance between design for easy analysis and the opportunity for people to freely express their views, in terms of stating their expectations as well as their current impressions. These and related key requirements for a good survey are discussed in more detail below.

QUESTION DESIGN

A survey typically consists of a number of questions to which people are expected to respond by choosing from a given set of answers. This is not true of all surveys, of course; some are designed to allow free-form text answers to each question to provide maximum opportunity for gathering information and collecting ideas. These have their place, but their usefulness as a measuring tool for surveying employees is highly limited since it is very difficult to allocate scores on a fixed scale to infinitely variable answers. This means that, when trying to measure, the first thing to understand is that the questions should all be multiple choice and ideally, as mentioned in Chapter Five, incorporate a set of guidelines to the employee on exactly how to position their answer within the given choices.

My own preference is to make the questions and their answer sets seem as different from each other as possible. It is very tempting to define a standard set of answers to a question such as:

- Extremely satisfied
- Very satisfied
- Quite satisfied
- A little dissatisfied
- Very dissatisfied
- Extremely dissatisfied

and then to list this set of options against every question. While it does have the advantage of making it easier for the employee to read and follow and much easier to subsequently analyse, those completing the survey could easily decide just to adopt a pattern and decide, for example, to rush through the form ticking 'a little dissatisfied' against every question. Even where they do vary their responses, having standard answers all the way through reduces the real thought that is given to every question. Although a set like this can be quite useful, it is probably best to phrase the questions differently to provide sufficient variation to make respondents think about each question. So, for example, one question such as 'How satisfied are you with the quality of food from the canteen?' might have the answer set shown above, while another question asking 'Do you think that current weekly team briefing meetings are . . . ?' might have the following answer set:

- Ridiculously long
- Too long
- A little too long
- About right
- A little too short
- Much too short.

This requires the respondent to think much more carefully about how to answer the different questions. It also allows you to tailor the answers towards the question – for example, a simple set of satisfaction answers in response to the second question would not tell us whether a person was dissatisfied because they thought the meeting too long or because it was too short.

It may be a good idea, however, to have the same answer set to some questions, where appropriate. For example, if some questions are grouped and analysed together, that analysis may be difficult if the questions have different answer sets.

CHOICE OF SCALE

The choice of scale for the answer set is quite important. It must not be so large that the choice seems cumbersome or irrelevant (for example, it may be difficult to choose between 50 and 51 on a scale of 1 to 100, and writing detailed selection criteria for 100 points would be a nightmare). Neither must it be so short that it fails to provide for any variation in responses. Personally I would opt for 6 to 10 points.

Whether there should be an odd or even number of points also needs to be considered. Scales with an odd number of points allow people to select the middle ground, which may be a tempting option if they wish to be non-committal. I prefer an even number of points, as this forces the respondents to choose one side or other of the middle.

It is also a good idea to include a 'not applicable' option to the scale of answers. When quantifying the response this can be counted as a zero, with the analysis tool (often a spreadsheet) tuned to ignore zeros both in terms of the response and the numbers of people responding. This allows people to positively identify that a question does not apply to them – for example, questions relating to supervision where the person concerned does not supervise anybody. The alternative is to simply allow them not to answer irrelevant questions, but then the dilemma is posed at each unanswered item: is it unanswered because it is not applicable or is it just because they did not want to answer it? The best approach is to have a 'not applicable' category and suggest to respondents that they should answer every question.

> **TIP**
> Final analysis will be much simpler if the same number of points is selected for each answer scale, even though the description of the points may differ for every question.

NUMBER OF QUESTIONS

Obviously one of the main things that affects the number of questions is the range of topics that needs to be covered. Equally important, however, is that there should be a number of questions for each topic. Although it might seem simple and direct just to ask a straightforward question in each area of interest, this approach is not really subtle enough to produce good results.

Imagine a survey one of whose objectives is to find out whether people think that they are being adequately communicated with. If we simply state 'Communication from my team leader is excellent' and give a number of levels of agreement as possible responses, we can almost guarantee that we will receive a generally dissatisfied answer to our survey question. On the other hand, if we had a number of statements of the type:

- My team leader speaks to me about what is going on in the organization at least once a week
- My team leader explains the purpose behind tasks and responsibilities that I am assigned
- My team leader provides me with key information that I need as soon as is practicable

then we are likely to obtain much more useful answers. I use ten questions as my own standard in such cases, aiming to provide a good spread, but a manageable number, of questions on the same topic.

GROUPING OF QUESTIONS

Once we have decided to use several questions to cover each topic that we wish to investigate, we then need to understand the best way of laying them out in the questionnaire. The obvious approach is to provide a series of headings on the questionnaire form that describe the topics in turn and list the individual questions under them. The problem with this is that it rather defeats the object. The reason that we have multiple questions is to prompt respondents to answer each one correctly and factually, rather than from an overall impression of the topic. If, however, it is clear that all questions are aimed at one objective, the temptation remains to think of one's overall impression of the subject and mark every question according to that impression.

A better approach is first to define the questions that relate to each specific topic and then perform the equivalent of putting them into a cocktail shaker and mix them all up. Thus if we have ten overall topics represented by 100 questions, the questions for the first topic might be numbered 1, 14, 16, 24, 41, 57, 59, 83, 87 and 97. These are simply presented in numerical order on the questionnaire with no topic headings given. Those answering the questionnaire are then simply asked to deal with a question on its own merits rather than under topic headings, resulting in a much clearer and more honest set of answers. We can then perform the analysis both on the individual questions, as well as by pulling them together to indicate the response to the overall topic, without preconditioning the individual answers to give just one single level of response. This is exactly the technique employed in psychological profiling, used successfully for exactly the same reasons as given for using it with employee measurement surveys.

> **TIP**
> When designing the questionnaire, remember to keep a careful note of which questions relate to which topic. I once encountered a designer who forgot to do so, and it was very difficult to unravel it later.

GAP IDENTIFICATION

Surveys cannot identify behaviours amongst people, only feelings and opinions. This represents a disadvantage since we have earlier suggested that behaviours are most important, but it can also be a useful tool for identifying, for example, underlying reasons for undesirable behaviour. Because of this, internal employee surveys will typically ask about a variety of things that might indicate how people feel and where their opinions are strongest. Since, however, different people will feel differently about different things, it also means that some people will care more about some aspects of the organization's work than others.

It is vital to consider how much people care about things in direct relation to how good they think the situation is in the organization. The solution is to ask the survey respondents to answer each question twice – first, for how well they think the organization is performing in each aspect and, second, for how important they think it is. So, for example, the statement earlier in this chapter 'My team leader speaks to me about what is going on in the organization at least once a week' may have a set of possible choices in terms of measuring the respondent's agreement with the statement and then another set, with a scale of the same size, asking for their impression of its importance. The resultant section of the questionnaire may then look something like that shown in Table 6.1.

Having this dual set of answers provides us with a much better result than only a single set. To explain this, let us look at two possible opposite examples. In the first we might ask how much effort the organization appears to devote to supporting the local community and obtain an answer 'not very much'. This might seem to indicate a requirement for corrective action, but if the answer to the importance section reveals that people do not consider it important (for example, they may feel that it is not the job of commercial organizations to perform community service) then our people measurement programme may not indicate that we need to do anything at all. By contrast, the survey may reveal that employees feel that the organization is quite good at allowing flexibility in timekeeping in the case of domestic crises and so on but, if the importance is rated at the top of the range as 'essential', there is probably still some room for improvement.

Table 6.1 Situation and importance answers

Statement	Current situation	Level of importance
My team leader speaks to me about what is going on in the organization at least once a week	• Absolutely agree • Strongly agree • Agree • Mostly agree • Slightly disagree • Strongly disagree • Not applicable to my work	• Vital • Extremely important • Very important • Quite important • Don't feel strongly • Don't wish to be informed • Not applicable to my work

When analysing and subsequently reporting the results of a survey, we become interested in two numbers: the employees' impression of the overall performance level in each topic area and the gap between performance and importance figures (which can also be seen as the difference between actual and desired performance). This is calculated by deducting the perceived performance number from the importance number. The importance number is not interesting in itself, but is highly revealing when considered in relation to the reported performance level. In fact, the gap figure is arguably the most useful of all since it tells us where the biggest shortfalls are. A negative gap figure tells us that our employees are probably quite satisfied with how things are being managed, but the larger positive values indicate areas that require the attention of the organization's leaders.

Take care not to rely solely on the gap results, though. Areas in which the overall performance is perceived to be low may well be important, even if the majority of employees do not report it as such. After all, the designer of the survey must have considered the issue important enough to want to include it in the questionnaire. For instance the importance of accurately reporting all costs may not be recognized by many employees but is essential to the effective control of any large organization.

APPLICATION AND COVERAGE

Employee surveys are usually large, time-consuming and disruptive affairs – necessarily so, in order to do their job properly. I have occasionally seen them run as very simple exercises with only a few questions that can be completed in less than five minutes (the standard questionnaires that used to be employed at the start of UK Investors in People programmes are a case in point), but such small efforts in questionnaire design tend to produce small efforts from the respondents. A small survey tends to be viewed as not very important and will be paid little attention. The same is true of the managers who will look at the results afterwards; an apparently minor and trivial survey will not be taken very seriously.

The point that I made earlier about having a number of questions against each topic should also be borne in mind. If we wish to learn only three things from the workforce, this will result in approximately 30 questions and will take much more than a few seconds of casual thought to answer.

Once we have determined that the survey is likely to be a large exercise it is both a shame and pointless to waste the effort. Consequently, we should aim to cover every element of the workforce in the exercise. The survey should be given to everyone that works in the organization, and every single person should be actively encouraged to complete it fully. Being really active is the key. The benefits of the survey must be promoted (see below) and a timescale set. Then people should be continually reminded that they need to return their completed forms, both before and after the deadline is due (assuming that some allowance is made in the timescale for those who do not return their forms before the initial milestone).

It is also important that all categories of employees are included. I have been a frequent visitor to a major Anglo-American company where the staff all introduce themselves to me as either permanent or contract, a clear distinction that is obviously important within the organization. Yet, in reality, employing contractors is only a device that enables the company to rid itself of personnel with only short tenure more easily. In terms of their contribution to the overall business and what work they do, makes little actual difference. No survey, then, should make a distinction between such categories of employees; everybody should be included, from full-time permanent employees to those on part-time temporary contracts. Excluding them could do greater damage to morale and teamwork than would be justified and would result in a less realistic picture from the survey results.

PROMOTING THE USAGE

As mentioned above, it is important that everyone completes the questionnaire in order to make it viable. If we send it out, but only half the employees bother to return it we have an unrepresentative set of answers (some might argue that the answers might be representative of a particular sector of the population, but there can be numerous unpredictable reasons why people will not answer surveys).

PROTECTING THE RIGHT TO FREE EXPRESSION

One of the prime barriers to answering survey questions, or at least to answering them honestly, is the fear of incrimination. People suspect that, if they give answers that appear to criticize the corporate leadership, they will be marked as troublemakers, or at least will be asked to explain their answers to their supervisor. If this fear is allowed to remain, people will either fail to return their questionnaires or will give bland, uncontroversial answers designed to protect their own skins.

The only answer to this is anonymity. If survey forms are returned with no indication of who completed the questionnaire, people can answer truthfully and fully without fear of their answers coming back to haunt them via management recriminations. This means that the forms must have no space for the name of the respondent and there needs to be an anonymous collection mechanism, such as a central post box or simple use of the internal mail. Any risk of even accidental identification of the respondent should be eliminated; in a small organization, handwriting can be a give-away and simple crosses or a similar device in multiple-choice format should be used.

This does have some disadvantages. It can be useful to categorize responses by origin – by department, job grade, specialization and so on. Yet if anonymity is to be preserved it is impossible to identify such things for risk of the specifics pinpointing the individual (a grade 6 supervisor in the technical services department can probably be only one of two people and if we add the duration of service with the company then it is quite clear who they are). Only in the largest of organizations can we gather such demographical information without destroying anonymity.

Another disadvantage of anonymity is that it may encourage people to express excessive venom; if they are having a bad day they may be tempted to be more strongly critical of the organization and its leaders than they would otherwise be, knowing that they have complete immunity. In other words, the pendulum of freedom of expression may swing so far that maliciousness is let loose.

Another practical, but key, disadvantage is that it is not possible to identify those who have not yet returned their questionnaires; hence we are unable to chase them up to remind them to return them and nor is it possible to tell whether the survey is unbalanced because, for example, one group of people, such as a specific department, has declined to complete their forms.

On balance, though, the benefits of anonymity outweigh the drawbacks. It will at least encourage people to feel that they can be honest and might promote a better rate of questionnaire return.

ENCOURAGING BELIEF

Another key factor in ensuring that people respond to a survey is encouraging them to believe that it is worthwhile. If the prevailing opinion is that real action will be taken on the basis of the survey results, employees will probably be more keen to respond to the survey and will do so diligently. If they believe it to be yet another half-hearted fad or some cynical ploy to manipulate the workforce, they may either not bother to fill it in at all or only half-heartedly think about the answers.

All this means that some advance preparation must be carried out. First, management must be convinced that taking action on the concerns of employees is the right thing to do. They must also be mentally prepared for the fact that some of the required actions may seem costly or painful, but will be necessary because the workforce is concerned about them.

Second, they must ensure that funds are available to take the necessary actions. It will not be possible to budget specific amounts since it cannot be foreseen what exactly will need to be done, but understanding that some expenditure will be necessary is important.

Third, there should be an appointed champion who will promote the programme and sell its benefits to the intended respondents; the champion must be somebody who is believed and trusted by the workforce, otherwise the project will fail. (Of course, leaders in all aspects of business have problems if they are not trusted, but sadly there are still some managers who do not engender trust in their workforce, and such people must not be selected as measurement champions.)

Finally, all of this needs to be communicated to the target audience. Not only must managers learn to accept the survey analsyis and be prepared to spend some money as a result, but they must also convince the workforce that they have learnt these lessons. This will require a comprehensive communication programme during the run-up to the survey questionnaire. It is not sufficient just to announce that a survey will be conducted and then issue it the next day. Successful programmes will often have countdowns to the day when the questionnaire is issued, explaining some new detail at each stage but also reinforcing the overall message of how important it is and how committed the company is to acting upon what it reveals.

RUNNING A SURVEY

Carrying out the survey is a project much like any other; it requires coordination of all activities so that they are done correctly, within budget and on time. These three objectives of a project are often stated as quality, cost and delivery. I shall deal with each of them below.

QUALITY

Quality means that it must be right. The programme requires integrity and adherence to the aims and principles embodied in the original motives for the survey. One of the key things to keep in mind here is not to sacrifice the principles for expediency or guile. So, for example, nobody should surreptitiously try to identify who the respondents are when the survey was intended to be anonymous. And, even though it may be tempting to press ahead with the analysis if we have what seems to be a sufficient number, nor should the last stragglers be ignored if they have not returned their questionnaires within the stated time – after all, those giving most thought and attention to the project may well take longer than those who simply glance over the questions.

If a rule or guideline for the survey is agreed in advance it must be adhered to, otherwise there is a great risk of the project failing, either through basic errors or lack of support. Therefore those running it must be clearly focused on quality. When we are busy it is often tempting to sacrifice what we think is right for what is easy or quick, but this inevitably leads to later difficulties which would not have arisen if we had done things properly in the first place. This truism relates just as well to running an employee survey as it does to making a product, planning an event or any other management initiative. We can ensure that we perform the survey well by having defined approaches to various tasks – much of this is addressed in the later chapters of this book.

COST

It will have to be recognized that an employee survey will cost time and money to run. The four main phases will each have their own costs: design, promotion, analysis and action.

The design phase is potentially the most expensive, both in management time and real money. It requires selling the idea to the management team, as well as composing a good questionnaire and its associated analysis tools. In many cases, this may involve employing an external consultant who can assist by providing direct experience plus an independent viewpoint, or perhaps buying a standard survey and paying to have it tailored to your own needs – either of which costs money.

> **TIP**
> Never buy a standard survey and use it unmodified. It will be unlikely to fit your organization well, and its origins may be obvious to those involved who will thus feel poorly motivated towards it.

Of course, the design can be totally created in-house if suitable confidence and ability exist; this will cost less money but will take more time. The benefits or otherwise of this approach will then depend on the urgency of the exercise and how the time of the developers is accounted for in your organization. If done well, however, it can result in something that is far more closely tailored to what you need than a questionnaire purchased from outside.

The promotion phase will also take time, and possibly some money to print promotional leaflets, run meetings or events and so on. Larger direct costs could be involved if the advising consultant or the firm from whom the survey has been bought are retained to help convince the workforce that it is a good idea. Similarly, analysis, although requiring no purchase of promotional material, is very time-consuming and may involve buying an analysis tool (such as a piece of software, either off-the-shelf or developed specifically).

Taking subsequent action can be the most expensive phase. Ideally, the main actions that arise from a well managed employee survey will produce long-term financial benefits resulting from reduced staff turnover, better attendance, improved work rates and practices and so on. Few of these, however, will result in immediate cost savings. In the short term, the project will cost money through expenditure on schemes to address the concerns raised by the survey. This may mean refurbishment of rest areas, provision of vending machines, increased training provision or anything else that needs to be done to correct the problems identified from the analysis. This must be budgeted for and understood by all as an essential ingredient of the survey. Spending money to put right fundamental flaws in employee relations is not a waste of money; funds are only wasted if an employee survey is conducted and then nothing is done about the results because the organization's leadership is too shortsighted to spend the money.

Monitoring cost

Monitoring cost is one of the key responsibilities of the survey's project manager or champion. A budget should be set in advance for running the survey and tackling the most urgent concerns. The project manager will need to have a simple way of keeping track of what is being spent and where overspend might occur, being prepared to go back to the holders of the purse strings if necessary and seek further funds in the light of developments. Unless your organization's activities are strongly project-based and, as a result, there is a familiar and accepted information system for tracking project costs, my experience is that simple forms, or perhaps spreadsheets, are best, rather than trying to adapt accounting systems that are not really intended for the purpose.

One of the most important aspects of this is monitoring the charges incurred through the use of external experts or consultants. When using such external resources it is easy for costs to run away. The worst scenario is where the consultant is given relatively free rein and simply charges by the day or hour for as long and as much as they decide is necessary; this can happen where those commissioning the work do not have the knowledge, experience or time to adequately specify and control the project, leaving it to the consultant to do what they wish. Even where the consultant's time is limited, there is still the danger that large 'extras', such as travelling expenses or other supporting costs, will be charged.

Consultants must be managed by giving them a clear brief with firm objectives and fixed timescales (exactly as is done in any professional project). The agreement must specify what is to be done, by when and the *maximum* amount of bookable time that the consultant can spend in achieving the objectives. This demonstrates the total commitment of the organization. If the consultant needs to spend more time than was originally proposed, through no fault of yours, they should be expected to do this at no charge. The progress towards objectives (such as the achievement of key milestones) should be monitored by the project manager and compared to the amount of time booked by the consultant so far. This approach should also adopted for expenses and charges for 'extras'; ideally, the charges should be included in the quoted fees but, if this cannot be done, the nature of, and formula for, expense charging must be agreed in advance and, again, maximum figures defined.

I am not suggesting that using consultants is a bad idea or will always result in unnecessarily high costs. They can be a very cost-effective way of running this sort of project, especially where management time is limited. In order to make them cost-effective, though, they must be well managed and controlled; it has been reported that the most common cause of dissatisfaction with the use of consultants is the failure to adequately define the nature of the work to be done and to take control of the cost of the work.[1]

DELIVERY

Delivery equates to the timing of the various activities. Ensuring that each step of the programme occurs at the right time is essential to its success. First, there is the obvious consideration that if

---

1. *Dangerous Company*, J. O'Shea and C. Madigan, Nicholas Brealey Publishing, 1997.

elements do not fall into place on time there will be delays which, in turn, are likely to increase costs. However, there are two other key reasons why making things happen at the right time is important:

- Delays could make the gathered data no longer relevant, or mean that a portion of the data is gathered under different conditions than the rest, rendering the whole exercise invalid.
- If the programme is not adhered to, respondents will lose faith in the process and the promises made by the organization's management.

Keeping track of timing is one of the most traditional project management tasks. There is a wide variety of techniques and tools for helping to manage timing – I find that simple project barcharts (sometimes known as Gantt charts) are the best for this purpose. For those not familiar with the techniques, a simple book such as Dennis Lock's *Essentials of Project Management*[2] will prove a useful source of information.

ANALYSING THE RESULTS

From an administrative viewpoint, analysing the results of the survey is much simpler than obtaining replies to the questionnaire. All the data is in one place and only a small number of people is involved, as opposed to the entire workforce that participates in the actual gathering of data. Technically, though, it is a much more complex activity since it is never clear exactly how the results should be treated and reported until we have been through a few iterations.

AVERAGES

The first way of treating a series of numbers that springs to most of our minds is to average them, so let us deal with that first.

There are three types of average: mean, mode and median. The mean is the sum of the total sample values, divided by the sample size (that is, the scores for each person for one question added together, then divided by the number of people replying). The mode is the value most often encountered (that is, the score given most frequently by respondents). The median is the midpoint between the highest and lowest values encountered in the sample (that is, the figure obtained by adding the lowest score to a question given by any respondent to the highest score for that question, then dividing by 2).

MEAN

The mean is the most commonly used form of average, as described in Chapter One. It should also be the first form of analysis used in an employee survey. It should be used to report:

- the mean score for each question
- the mean score for each category of questions (that is, the mean for all questions in that category)
- the mean importance score for each question
- the mean importance score for each category of questions.

From these four sets of numbers can also be derived the 'gap' (representing the difference between the desired mean value and the satisfaction mean value) for both individual questions and categories. In theory it is this gap figure which is the most interesting when it comes to deciding what action to take.

Bear in mind that the number of people responding to a question can affect the mean. For example, if only one person answers, the data will by totally influenced by that individual's feelings

---

2. *The Essentials of Project Management*, D. Lock, Gower Publishing, 1996.

whereas, if 1000 people answer, individual feelings will be lost in the whole. For this reason it is worth, against each mean value reported, noting the number of people who answered that question (since there will inevitably be some people that answer some points on the questionnaire but leave others blank). If you give an option to say 'I don't know' or 'not relevant' in response to a question and score it as zero, remember to make sure that your analysis technique ignores zeroes when considering the number of respondents, otherwise the data will become skewed. (Most spreadsheet packages can be set to do this very easily, if that is the tool you are using.)

These mean values can provide a reasonable insight into how the workforce as a whole feels. It only gives us generalizations, though. For example, a workforce that is uniformly reasonably content might all provide a score of 3 from a scale of 1 to 5, giving a mean of 3; yet a workforce that is deeply divided might provide half the answers as 5 and half as 1, still providing a mean of 3. The results are identical but the circumstances are obviously completely different. When applied to a group of questions this effect is enhanced, since we are making generalizations in a much broader set, so although having these figures is useful, we need to understand their limitations.

Mode

The modal average is another way of looking at the response of the largest number of people. Because it reports what people actually said on their questionnaire, it overcomes the disadvantage of means which can produce a value that nobody actually agrees with (for example, if three people surveyed respond with 1, 1 and 4, then the mean is 2 but nobody actually thinks that 2 is the right answer). It does have its own disadvantages, however, the main one being that it takes no account of any data other than those at the modal value. In the example given earlier in this paragraph, the mode is 1, which ignores the fact that a third of the values are much higher.

The mode is best reported alongside the mean to provide increased information. The four modal values corresponding to the four mean values listed above should also be calculated for the answer both individually and by group, and each displayed in the final report against the means.

> **TIP**
> Do not try to calculate modal gaps in the same way that mean gaps are used; the fact that modes make no use of some of the collected data means that gap calculations are relatively meaningless.

Median

I have a heading for medians here because they are another type of average and therefore I need to mention them, but for our purposes medians have no real use. Knowing the midpoint of answers to employee survey questionnaires tells us nothing, so I suggest that they are not used to analyse the results.

RANGES

In order to overcome the problem that averages do not say much about the spread of results, it is a good idea also to look at the range of the data collected. Range represents the spread of results from the lowest to the highest and thus indicates to what degree the workforce is speaking with one voice, or whether opinions widely differ.

At its simplest, the range is calculated by subtracting the lowest value reported from the highest (ignoring zeroes, of course, since these are an artificial value). So if a scale of 1 to 5 were being used, a range of 4 would suggest that we have the full spectrum of opinions whereas a range of 2 would indicate that people are much more in agreement about the state of affairs.

This can be very useful for small populations. If we are only surveying a workforce of, say, 20 people, this information could be quite revealing. Obviously, however, if the size of the population that is being surveyed is larger the spread of opinions will become more varied and we would quickly find that the range of every question or group always came out as 4, which would tell us nothing.

This means that, for larger populations, we need a more sophisticated indication of range – one that gives us an idea of how many people are responding at the mean level and how many at the extremes. For instance, the range would be 4 if, from a population of 100, 98 people answered 2, one answered 1 and one answered 5, but simply reporting the range as 4 would not tell us that it was only two mavericks who did not respond at the mean level.

One way of overcoming this difficulty would be to report all values for each question, possibly in barchart form, as shown in Figure 6.1.

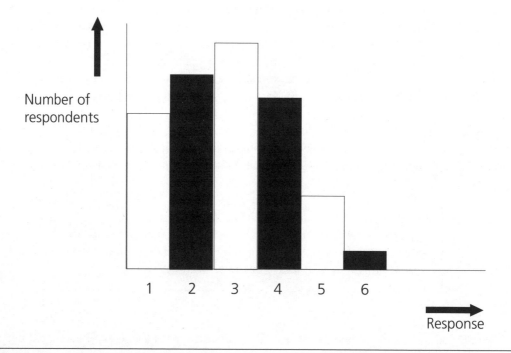

Figure 6.1   Barchart of all reported values

This figure shows us the pattern of responses; the barchart form allows us to see the sort of spread involved without bogging us down with the actual numbers. This can be a useful method, but is frankly very time-consuming to prepare and read for anything other than the smallest of surveys. In practice I suggest that this is only done when the organization's leaders decide that they wish to study the response to an individual question in some detail.

A more practical way of looking at spread is to use a statistical measurement known as standard

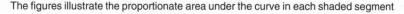

The figures illustrate the proportionate area under the curve in each shaded segment

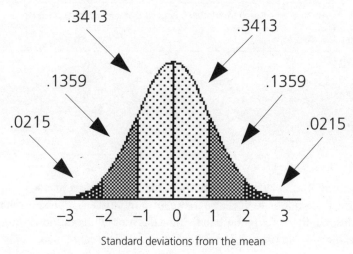

Standard deviations from the mean

Figure 6.2 Normal distribution

deviation. This is a quantification of how much a population is spread away from its mean value. In theory, it makes certain assumptions about the shape of the data, in that it can only be realistically interpreted for a 'normal' population – that is, one that has a shape akin to that shown in Figure 6.2.

Standard deviation is calculated by first determining the mean value of the population, then taking each point's variation from the mean, calculate the standard deviation using the following formula:

$$S = \sqrt{\frac{\Sigma (x-u)^2}{N}}$$

where:
s is the standard deviation
x is the individual value
u is the mean of the sample
N is the number of items in the sample

For those not particularly mathematically inclined, do not let this formula put you off, since most spreadsheets are happy to do this for you: simply select the set of data for which you wish to calculate the standard deviation, then choose the standard deviation option from the formula list and, hey presto, it is done.

A particular feature of this statistic is that it tells us something specific about the shape of our data. For a normal distribution, we know exactly how much of the data lies within certain distances from the mean value, as shown in Table 6.2.

For the purposes of employee surveys, much of this is only important as background information, providing an understanding of what standard deviation means. However, we can use it in our results analysis to see how well our overall results conform to the mean value. It is not necessary for the sample data to be distributed normally, since we are only concerned with comparison; if the standard deviation is higher in one area than the others, then we have a wide dispersion of responses to that

Table 6.2   Normal distribution coverage

Percentage covered by number of standard deviations from the mean	
Standard deviations	Percentage
0.674	50%
1	68.3%
1.645	90%
2	95.4%
2.576	99%
3	99.7%

question or group; if it is relatively small, then there is considerable agreement amongst the workforce. It is useful, therefore, to display a figure for standard deviation alongside the mean values for opinion and desirability scores for both individual questions and question groups.

Standard deviation is also used when testing for change in a set of data, as discussed in Chapter Ten.

INDIVIDUAL VALUES

Since there is likely to be a number of people in the surveyed organization, it is most useful to have the results displayed as mean, modes, ranges and standard deviations for the entire size of population surveyed. I have already explained, though, that such analysis has its limitations and represents limited information. In fact, if we truly wish to understand what has been reported by the workforce then we need to look at the raw data (just as in the film *The Matrix*, where the only way in which the Matrix could be truly interpreted was by looking at a straight representation of the data stream). Now, to present the individual data for each respondent to all managers for all questions and question groups would be unproductive since it would represent an information overload; this is why we use summary information such as averages. Where, however, the summaries indicate that a particular area requires investigation, it may be necessary to study the actual individual scores that have been given by each respondent. These cannot be reported simply as a list, since the data is impossible to assimilate unless the number of respondents is very small. A practical solution is to count the number of people giving each level of answer and produce a bar graph. The first step would be to create a tally; we could either use a traditional tally chart or, since we are likely to be using computer tools for any but the most basic of surveys, enter the data into a spreadsheet.

The first result of this analysis might then produce a table as indicated in Table 6.3. From this, we

Table 6.3   Individual survey response summary

Individual response summary to survey question no. 37	
Level of response	Number of people responding
5	17
4	43
3	37
2	10
1	2
0	1

could create a simple barchart showing the distribution of responses amongst individuals surveyed, giving a graph similar to that shown in Figure 6.1 (p. 70). This gives us a more detailed idea of how individuals responded for each question. Such tables and graphs can be vital information for managers who wish to understand the precise nature of response to any individual topic. Indeed, it may be a good idea for those conducting the analysis to prepare summary tables and graphs of this type for every question. Although, as stated earlier, detail would be too much to present to managers, it would be useful to have as a set of detailed data to offer, on request, to those who like to wade through reams of figures.

> **TIP**
>
> For any presentation or report, it is a good idea to have detailed information available separately, so that those who only want the basics do not need to see it but those who like to examine the minutiae are not disappointed.

ORGANIZATIONAL CATEGORIZATION

Another possible way of presenting the data can be by one or more means of organizational categorization. When we are looking at average, spread or individual data, it can be useful to understand from whence those data derive. Thus it may be useful to provide separate tables and graphs by:

- department
- function
- specialization
- status or level.

For example, it might be especially meaningful if the overall data revealing that the company appears to have a lack of direction and vision comes more strongly from management grades than others, or if sales and commercial functions feel that strong attention is paid to customers needs but nobody else thinks so (in this case, the positive respondents may be showing a defensive reaction whereas others are reporting a more accurate representation of the truth).

Again, such information may represent too detailed an analysis for many of those who wish to view the results but may be a useful set of background figures for those who are especially interested in looking at specific figures. Preparing the right divisional and category analysis can be useful to have ready for when it is, inevitably, demanded by the appropriate personnel.

Of course, as we have already discussed, this categorization can only be undertaken in a large organization where anonymity is not risked by collecting the information in this way. Anonymity is highly desirable and should be protected as a priority, even if it means sacrificing the ability to analyse results by organizational category.

TOOLS

For all types and sizes of organization, you will need some sort of tool to help analyse and present the data. If the size of population surveyed is very small, it may be possible to have something as simple as a set of standard forms and tables on which to write the results and perform any calculations that might be necessary. In an organization of any size, however, you are almost certain to need some sort of computer software that will make the task simpler, quicker and more elegant.

At one end of the spectrum, you could invest in a bespoke program written specifically for survey analysis. Certainly if you employ external consultants to help with the project, they may well expect to use such a tool – either a standard version or one written specifically for the specific survey – for treating the results. Be cautious about adopting such a solution, however, and make sure that you understand how the program is crunching the numbers before going ahead and using the data; simply accepting both the tool and its output can result in damaging misinterpretation of results.

The obvious tool for those needing to employ something a little more sophisticated than paper forms but not wishing to invest in a suite of programs is to design a spreadsheet for the purpose. Modern spreadsheet programs are highly versatile and easy to use, and most organizations have at least one person who is highly skilled at coming up with a spreadsheet to fulfil specific needs (or, if not, at least has access to such a person). Spreadsheets can easily be shaped to analyse the results, calculate averages, gaps, standard deviations and so on, and present the final output as a chart or graph. The figures shown in this book were all initially generated using a spreadsheet. Again, it is possible that external advisers will have their own predesigned set of spreadsheets for the purpose. Although this will make the job easier, remember to check first how the tool treats the data to ensure that the output is correctly understood.

Whatever tool is used, it is important to design it before the feedback forms start to roll in and the analysis needs to be done. That way it can be validated in advance and the danger of tweaking the tool to produce the desired, rather than actual, outcome, can be reduced.

TIP

When using any computer-based analysis tool, always create a small set of dummy data and run it through the program before the real project starts, just to check that output makes sense.

SUMMARY

- Surveys typically rely on a questionnaire with large numbers of questions.
- Questions should be grouped for easier analysis.
- Running the survey regularly can help to make best use of results, as long as it is not done too often.
- The available responses should change from question to question to avoid thoughtless answers.
- A scale of 6, 8 or 10 possible answers is best, with an additional '0' option for those to whom the question is not applicable.
- There should be a reasonable number of questions – say ten – per topic that we wish to consider.
- Questions on a single topic should be sprinkled randomly throughout the questionnaire.
- Respondents should be asked how desirable or important each item is, so that the gap between desirability and perceived actual performance can be measured.
- As far as is practicable, all employees of all types and at all levels should participate in the survey to enable a full picture to be obtained.
- People should be able to respond freely without fear of recrimination.
- Anonymity of response helps to ensure truthful answers.

- Everybody must be encouraged to believe that it is a worthwhile exercise to help make the programme a success.
- When analysing the results, calculating means, modes, gaps, ranges and total numbers of respondents are all useful inputs to the final picture.
- Looking at the actual individual responses can also be useful in areas that apparently need attention.
- If possible, classifying responses based on their place in the organization can provide extra information, but this should not be done at the expense of anonymity.
- Formal tools can be designed or purchased for questionnaire analysis, but standard spreadsheets are usually more than capable of carrying this out.

CHAPTER SEVEN

Measurement by Interview

THE INTERVIEW TECHNIQUE

The employee interview is the primary tool of the method that I referred to in Chapter Five as 'second-party assessment'. Unlike the survey, which relies on employees themselves to determine the level of their feelings and performance, it uses an expert who can interpret what the employees say and turn their words into something that more directly relates to the measurement programme's objectives.

This type of measurement programme is most commonly employed by external consultants. As well as employing it to support the management's measurement initiative, they can use it to help them design their own programme of work or give them insights into how the company is run or managed that could not be obtained just by talking to the managers. Indeed, an interview programme is very difficult to run without external experts. For it to be successful, the interviewer has to be seen by the employee as completely independent; if there is any fear that the answers given will be used against the individual, then the interview will not be open and communicative. Employees who are nervous about what it is safe to say will only give partial answers and 'the truth' will thus not be forthcoming. Perhaps in a very large organization there could be some remote position that people will accept as being totally 'straight' and reliable, but in smaller companies any person conducting the interviews will always be known to be part of one interest group or another and thus will generate suspicion amongst at least some of the people being interviewed.

The main purpose of the interview technique is to read between the lines. As I shall explain below, in order for it to work, the interview programme has to be set up so that each person is asked the same set of questions. Instead of simply trying to place the answers within a numerical scale, however, the analysts (usually members of the interview team), seek to interpret what is meant by the manner and style of the answer, as well as its actual content. This is where face-to-face interviews can score over many other people measurement methods and can produce a wide range of information. As mentioned in Chapter Five, there are some programmes in which interviews are used just to obtain a simple, quantifiable answer or response. This can be a valid measurement but is really only an extension of the questionnaire survey technique and is, therefore, not the subject of our attention here.

> TIP
> If what you are looking for is simply an answer from a list, such as always/often/sometimes/rarely/never, the survey or monitoring techniques are easier and less intrusive than interviews.

IMPACT

Information gathering by interview is also the highest profile of the three people measurement styles that are discussed in this book. Although everybody will notice that they have been sent a questionnaire, the amount of attention that they give to completing it may be rather small. Many may view it as just another piece of paper (or e-mail) that has no more impact than all the other messages that cross their desk or workplace every day. Even worse, it could be perceived in the same light as all the customer satisfaction surveys with which many of us are constantly bombarded and of which the majority will be consigned to the wastepaper basket. The constant monitoring style of measurement may not be noticed at all by those being measured, especially if they are not privy to, or particularly interested in, the results.

When a series of interviews are being carried out, however, with the possible attendant visits of independent interviewers and people constantly stepping in and out of closed rooms for private and confidential discussions, it is hard to miss, especially if the interview net is spread to cover as many employees as possible. This can be important if the company wishes to make the exercise highly visible to show how much they value and act upon the feelings and performance of their people. On the other hand, if a low-key exercise is sought, this could represent a factor against deciding to run an interview programme.

CONTINUITY

There is a sense in which the interview method of people measurement is highly akin to the survey questionnaire – that is, it is a one-off project. In order to make valid measurements and comparisons, the interviews need to be conducted close together over as short a period as possible, then the results analysed. This ensures that the findings represent the circumstances at a certain time; if subsequent data is wanted, the exercise must be repeated to find out what the situation is at a later date. Consequently, the interview technique is not appropriate for measurements that need to be taken over a period of time or are intended to reveal rapidly evolving trends, particularly since the programme itself is likely to be too intrusive and disruptive to conduct too often.

PLANNING AN INTERVIEW PROGRAMME

There is much to consider when designing and planning an interview project. In fact, the list is potentially endless, depending on the level of detail into which one delves, just as with in any large project, and includes design, approval, scheduling, preparation, staffing and resources, budgets, facilities, rehearsal and validation (the last being particularly important since it is often forgotten).

DESIGN

One of the first planning issues to consider is the design of the interview project. The primary design work needed will be to define the interview process itself, together with the analysis method. This surprises many people new to the technique; after all, if this is to be a free interview, why should there be standard questions? Standard questions, they believe, will limit the conversation and are more appropriate to a survey questionnaire. Remember, however, that we are talking about a measurement project, in which we are trying to determine the workforce's position on a range of topics, rather than allowing employees to discuss subjects of their own choosing. In order to do this effectively, the same questions or prompts will need to be put to each person in a similar manner, so that the information obtained can be directly compared. If this is not done, there is a danger (some would say a certainty) that we will miss responses or input from some of the people interviewed and thereby damage the final results.

The difference between this technique and a set of survey questions is that there is no standard list of possible responses. The interviewee has to be free to talk openly and without restriction, so the quantification of what they say has to be done after the interview and not in response to individual questions. This does make the analysis more difficult, as discussed later in this chapter, but it does allow a far greater degree of freedom. Before the questioning can begin, however, the basic way in which the answers will be recorded and subsequently 'scored' must be defined so that there is some consistency (calibration) between individual interviews. This is even more important if there is to be more than one interviewer used, since there will then need to be common guidelines as to how to phrase questions (reading them directly from a sheet tends to make the interview rather stilted) and how to record and interpret the answers.

Other 'design' issues that will be dealt with before any interviewing can actually begin is the format of any standard documentation used, including any materials publicizing or giving details of the project. Some design considerations, such as the layout and style of the final report, can be left to a later stage and a judgement made based on the actual data and analysis, but anything affecting the conduct of the interviews themselves must be fully clarified before any of the sessions commence.

APPROVAL

For any exercise of this nature there must be a 'client' – that is, the person or group who wants it to take place and has initiated it within the organization. This client, or their representative, must be given the opportunity to comment on, and approve, the most important elements of the scheme. There are two main reasons for this, both designed to ensure that effort is not wasted. The first is to prevent the embarrassment of finding that the topics covered and the way in which they were investigated is not what the client had in mind. The second is to ensure that the client 'buys in' to the approach, so that they cannot dismiss the results or the methods used at a later stage simply because they do not like what the exercise has told them.

Approval should typically be sought for the questions to be asked, the analysis protocol, the timing, the interviewee selection process or list and the choice and training of interviewers. Managers involved in approving the process should be well aware that their approbation is not a rubber-stamping exercise. The process should involve discussion, amendment and fine-tuning until the 'client' is completely satisfied with how it will work. The sort of conversation that goes:

> 'Ah well you can't complain now because you did approve it'
> 'Yes, but I thought you were just asking me if it was okay in general to go ahead with the programme'

will not do anybody any good and could make the whole exercise worthless.

SCHEDULING

I shall discuss scheduling in more detail below, under 'Timing', but it is worth pointing out here that scheduling forms an important part of the planning process. Knowing how long the various components will take, in which order they should happen and when they will occur is essential for smooth operation of the programme. If this is not planned in advance, the good timing practices that I discuss later will be difficult to attain.

Remember, though, that any complex project scheduling can never be fully accurate and is unlikely to be fully adhered to over a protracted period. Changes and problems are bound to arise during the project and these will require adjustments and compromises. Those running the interview project will have to remember to be innovative and flexible.

TIMING

Getting the timing right is crucial to a good interview project. The first aspect is to obtain the right balance between planning, preparation, conducting the interviews and performing the analysis.

PLANNING TIME

It is almost impossible to spend too long on planning. After all, the project does not have to be announced to the workforce at large until the interviews are about to start, so it does not really matter if the planning is lengthy.

The reason why it is good to take a long time is that adequate preparation can save both time and embarrassment (due to error) during the interview process itself and during subsequent analysis. If we know what will happen, when and by whom then we are more likely to save time and trouble later. Of course, it is not appropriate to take too long; sometimes teams can insist on spending excessive amounts of time in planning and preparation ('We're just not ready yet; we need a bit longer') as an excuse for fear or hesitation. The secret is to set, in advance, adequate time for full preparation and then require the project team to adhere to the timetable.

INTERVIEW TIME

There are two aspects to correct interview time: conducting the interviews at the correct moment in the programme, and keeping them to the right length.

Choosing the moment

As with any other project, performing the various tasks at the scheduled time is important for the timeliness of the whole undertaking. Any delays to one interview or set of interviews will often (not always, but usually) cause a delay to the overall project and are, therefore, always undesirable.

There are also other reasons for performing the interviews at the right time. One of the most significant is not practical, but political. If the project does not proceed on time, the workforce will see it being of lower priority than other jobs which are done on time and it will, therefore, have less credibility. It can be particularly irritating for people who have 'psyched themselves up' for an interview only to have it cancelled or postponed.

Another factor is the validity of the data. Planning should allow for interviews to be conducted as close together as possible, but at the same time seek to avoid times when temporary factors could affect the results – for example, during times of high stress for one or more functions (such as during the annual audit for the finance department) or close to events that could provide short-term variations in feeling and opinion (such as directly following the annual corporate pay review). On the other hand, if the interviews are delayed for some reason, this could affect the overall results by allowing undesirable factors to enter or by causing one set of data to be unrepresentative because the same underlying circumstances differ from those of another group of people.

The point in the overall programme at which to schedule the actual interviews is also critical. A common mistake is to be eager to start the interviews too early. If they are conducted before the team is truly ready then there is a strong danger that they will be poorly thought out and badly handled. Sufficient time needs to have been allowed to make sure that the full set of questions has been created and validated, that the interviewers are fully prepared and practised and that foreseeable problems, objections and questions have been allowed for. Time is also needed to fully promote and publicize the programme, including time to allay any fears that the workforce might express. Conversely, the start must not be delayed so long, for the sake of waiting until everything is just right, that the employees become bored with the whole idea.

Once the interview sessions have begun, they should be completed within as short a space of time as possible. The shorter the whole programme, the better the quality of the data produced. To illustrate what I mean, imagine a set of interviews in an organization that has identification of team spirit as one of its primary objectives, since this has been identified as both a key success factor and an area of immediate concern. There are 132 employees and we have decided that we will be fully inclusive and interview every single one. We have employed an external consultant who suggests that, to allow for other work commitments and the need to write up notes in between each interview, one interview will take place every other working day. If this schedule is rigidly adhered to, and no holidays or illness interrupt the process, the interview schedule will take exactly one year to complete. During that year, some of the people interviewed at the beginning may well have left the organization, changes will have occurred in team structures, promotions and pay rises will have been awarded and targets will have been met or missed. As a result, data from interviews near the end of the cycle will be based on a quite different foundation to those at the beginning, and it will be impossible to treat the whole picture as a sensible set of contiguous data.

Interview duration

Correct timing of the duration of the interview is also crucial. Several factors need to be taken into account:

- There must be sufficient time for all the questions to be posed and answered – leaving some out will negate the value of the results.
- The duration should be geared towards what is practical for the interviewees to spend away from the workplace.
- It should not take so long that interviewees become bored or restless.
- Each interview should take a similar amount of time.

This last item is of great importance; the amount of time that is spent with each interviewee will quickly become public knowledge. Even if the duration of the interviews is not externally observed, those involved will certainly speak to each other. Any that spend a disproportionate amount of time in the interview will inevitably complain about it to their workmates; if the resultant conversation reveals disparities between durations then there will be an inevitable and rapid reaction against the discrepancy. It does not matter whether extended interview duration is seen as a good thing for the interviewee (in that their thoughts were perceived as being of especial importance) or a bad thing (they were seen as not being clever enough to deliver their thoughts succinctly or they were viewed as a case needing extra management effort), the knowledge that some people have been given more time than others will inevitably lead to resentment.

The key to guaranteeing consistent interview duration is practice. It is impossible to know how long it will take to ask a set of questions and properly discuss the answers, unless the interviewer has tried it out. It is also necessary to practise more than once; we all know that doing something once is not a sufficient basis for judging how well it will work. We cannot judge with any certainty the typical length of an interview until we have a large enough sample. So the answer is to practise it – with other interviewers acting employee roles, with external experts, other project team members, and indeed any and every person that is available to help hone the interviewer's skills and make a final decision on the time that should be allowed.

Once we know how long it should last, guidelines can be given to interviewers so that they can continually monitor how long they are taking and adjust their style and approach accordingly, while trying not to stifle or prolong the process unduly. It is a good idea to present interviewers with timetables showing several points or stages during the interview, together with an earliest and latest time that each point, including the final conclusion, should have been reached.

QUESTIONS

Defining the right set of questions for employee measurement by interview is much more difficult than setting the questions for a survey or finding the right measurement indicators for continuous monitoring. They need to be designed to probe as deeply and strongly into the issues as possible, without requiring the interviewers to be trained psychoanalysts and without appearing threatening to the interviewees.

QUESTION TOPICS

As with any form of business or organizational project, we should start with the overall corporate objectives. When planning an initiative, there is always the danger of starting considering what can be done and how to do it. The correct way, of course, is to consider what *should* be done, and only then ponder whether it can be done.

The first step, then – as I have previously stated for surveys and as I shall later point out for continuous monitoring – is to think about what the organization wishes to achieve. From that, we can consider the sorts of things that we are seeking from our employees that will contribute to these objectives. Only then can we ask ourselves whether there are sensible areas to explore which would illustrate those things. If we do not take the trouble to look at the project this way, we could end up with a set of topics that are perfectly measurable but are of no real interest to the organization's leaders (and remember, if those at the very front of the organization do not support the project it has little chance of success).

From this premise, we can go on to define the steps in setting questions, such as:

1. Identify the culture, aims and goals of the organization.
2. Determine how our people contribute towards those aims and goals.
3. Decide which of these can sensibly be discussed at interview.
4. Find questions that will produce useful information on those topics.
5. Test and refine the questions until there is a powerful, working set of interview points that will produce worthwhile results.

QUESTION CRITERIA

Setting the individual questions is not a simple task. Plenty of time should be allowed to discuss what they should be, think them over, refine them, test them and get them just right before practice, testing and other final details are embarked upon.

The first consideration is that the question should elicit responses related to the intended topic. The question must be sufficiently specific and focused to ensure that the interviewee is channelled towards an appropriate response. The way in which the question is worded and posed should make the topic clear and help prevent the interviewee going off at a tangent.

The interviewee also needs to understand what is being asked. Questions must be clear and unambiguous so that no time is wasted through having to clarify and explain their meaning. An even more important pitfall to avoid is being offered an answer thought by the interviewer to mean one thing but by the interviewee to mean another. For example, if the interviewer were daft enough to ask a question as vague as: 'What is your feeling about timekeeping?', then the respondent may well think that they are asking about how important it is for people to arrive for work on time (especially if she is always in early and is annoyed that others sometimes arrive late) although the question may relate to more general issues of timing during the working day, such as arriving punctually for meetings. The question needs to be phrased in such a way as to be clear and specific, without overlabouring the point.

Although questions need to be clear enough to avoid misunderstanding, they also have to be sufficiently brief to make certain that the detail alone does not become so great that it is confusing, or perhaps so lengthy that the interviewee simply loses interest. A good rule should be to keep questions as short as possible, then testing the first draft for other requirements but only extending it the minimum necessary for clarity and so on.

Much of question design has to satisfy the needs of the interviewee. It must be remembered, however, that this form of employee measurement depends heavily on the interviewer who has to put the message across adequately but, equally, has to be able to note and interpret the answers. For this reason, the feelings of the interviewer also have to be taken into account. In particular, the interviewer should be comfortable with the questions that they have to pose. All interviewers ought to be involved in the design of questions; if they have reservations about any of them, feeling that they will be embarrassing, improper or unprofessional, such questions should be avoided or redesigned.

Neither must the questions appear too personal to the interviewee. It is all very well ensuring that the interviewers are comfortable with the topics being raised but communication will be limited if the interviewee's sensibilities are not also taken into account.

In addition, questions must not be too vague. I have already said that questions should be specific enough for the interviewee to be able to respond to what is being asked, not to what they *think* is being asked. This also means that the project team must design the questions to address specific issues. It is no good thinking that we probably ought to have a question about the future of some sort in there, and just ask people at the end whether they are optimistic about the future, as the response will be meaningless for the purposes of analysis. Do we wish to know about the future of the company's profits, or its location, or its market share, or its growth, or something else? Or perhaps it is not the company that we are talking about at all, but the individual, or the social club, or the charismatic current leader, or the engineering team's entry in Robot Wars. By the future do we mean for the rest of this year, during the next three years, or the next ten? If we want answers to several of these questions, we will have to ask several questions targeted to the individual topic. A vague question will give us a vague, unhelpful response. Even if a single interviewee and interviewer pair have a common understanding of what is meant, if the overall topic is not specific it is likely that another pair might take a different approach.

Each question should be designed to produce as much information as possible. In one sense, all the other criteria that I have given so far are intended to achieve maximum information, so perhaps this is the corollary of all the other items, but I also see it as more than that. The way in which questions are set should aim not just to obtain the straightforward answer but also provide the opportunity to delve into what lies behind the person's feelings. It is extremely useful to discover that our chairman is scored at 85 per cent for leadership by the workforce, but it is even more interesting if we are also able to report supporting information such as: '... but I wish he would not be so hard on people who don't grasp things as quickly as he does' or '... and we need to find a way of injecting the same energy into projects even when the chairman is not personally involved'.

Questions should therefore not be aimed just at producing a numerical value – although this is extremely important too.

As far as is practicable, all questions should be acceptable and applicable to every interviewee. This is an essential part of interview design: that it must make sense for the whole target group. There is a danger that the interview design team, if drawn from too narrow a section of the workforce, will design the questions to be applicable to people just like themselves, making it irrelevant to many others. Similarly, if there is a hidden agenda and managers want to use the interviews to gain information about just one small portion of the workforce, the interviews may be designed accordingly – a fact that will quickly become apparent to those for whom the interview is not relevant. In order for people to answer fully, openly and truthfully, and for the process to be accepted as valid and useful, as much as possible of the interview needs to be applicable to every interviewee.

PHRASING

When designing an interview programme it is important to remember that the interviewer has to be able to make the discussion sound natural. That means that they must be able to put questions in a way that feels comfortable to them and seems to fit the tone of the interview. This becomes especially important as the interview progresses; the first question can be read from a sheet but the development of the interview will rely partly on its apparent similarity to a conversation, which means that the interviewer must choose their own way of ensuring that each question is answered. Otherwise, the interview becomes nothing more than an expensive and time-consuming form of employee survey.

Having said this, the overall way of phrasing the question is still important. Some questions can be misinterpreted if they are put in a slightly unfamiliar way or can even cause offence when otherwise benign. For this reason, the design team needs to pay attention to the way in which the questions are worded on the interviewer sheet. They should consider each question in turn and ask whether wording and expression during the interview could cause any misunderstanding or problems. If they find any potential difficulties, they should give interviewers specific guidance as to which are the critical questions and what sort of phrasing is not appropriate – in some cases, even insisting that the exact words used in the design are employed (in which case it is better to have these questions very near the beginning or end of the interview when the 'flow' is less pronounced).

CONDUCTING THE INTERVIEW

I have given some clues about how the interview should be conducted above under 'Questions'. Carrying out the interview is not just, however, about how the questions are phrased and timed.

ENVIRONMENT

The interview must be held away from the workplace, somewhere relaxed enough so that the interviewee does not feel self-conscious but also private, so that they are confident that they cannot be overheard. Sometimes the formality of a boardroom or conference room can be overpowering for some workers who would normally never be invited into them, so a smaller room with less forbidding connotations might be preferable.

The interviewer should be somebody with whom the person is familiar, yet not a person whom they in any way mistrust. This means that, in some organizations, there is almost no option other than to employ outsiders. Even the friendly personnel manager may well be tainted by last year's redundancies or the disciplinary hearing of a colleague, so somebody with no apparent axe to grind can be a great help if we wish people to open up and be honest.

If somebody external, such as a consultant, is used, it is best if they are not seen as a complete stranger at the start of the interview. Ideally, they should have visited on more than one previous occasion and met the people who they will be interviewing. If this is not practicable – as in a very large organization, for example – they should at least have stood up and introduced themselves at some of the group meetings or team briefings held to explain the project. The alternative is for the interviewee to enter the room thinking 'Who on earth are you?', which also leads to mistrust.

If possible, the interviewer should also pay attention to some of the niceties of room layout. The furniture should not be arranged in such a way that the interview feels too formal or confrontational. This means avoiding a layout where the interviewer sits behind a desk or table with the interviewee on the other side. Preferably there should be no table or desk between them, so that the interview feels more like a conversation than an examination. If possible, low, soft chairs should be made available to make the atmosphere even more relaxed, with the interviewer making notes in a pad on her lap rather than leaning on a table. In fact, these rules should apply to most interviews, including those for recruitment and appraisal; it always helps to minimize any unnecessary nervousness.

STRUCTURE

There are few set rules about how the interview should be structured. However, a typical basic pattern is:

- introduction
- beginning
- middle
- end
- close-out.

(My way of remembering this simple sequence is aperitif, soup, main course, pudding and coffee.)

The introduction should be a simple recap of what the interview is about and why it is being conducted. It should also include some guidelines and information for the interviewee: how long it will take, the fact that the interviewee can say what they like in complete confidence, what will be done with the results and so on.

For the following sections, it seems rather obvious to say that an interview, or anything else for that matter, has a beginning, middle and an end, but it is important to think about the structure of the interview in this fashion.

The beginning should be a gentle introduction to the subject with some simple, general questions that are easy for the interviewee to answer. The middle should then cover those areas that perhaps require more thought or are more controversial – these topics should only be covered once the interviewee is into their stride. The ending comprises a gentle winding down with more simple questions and a simple summing up, ensuring that the interviewee is given the opportunity to air anything that they feel has not been covered. A good interviewer always has a feel for where they are in the sandwich – whether they are in the meat in the middle or in one of the softer layers on either side.

The interview should also be properly closed; the interviewee needs to be properly thanked and informed (or reminded) of how the information gained will be dealt with, and the interviewer should recap the most important points arising from the discussions.

THE CONVERSATION

The interview is potentially a much stronger source of information than a paper questionnaire but in order to realize its benefits, the temptation to simply recite a few questions from the prepared sheet must be avoided. The conversation should be exactly that: a two-way communication between individuals and not one person using their own words to answer questions that are read out to them. This means that the interviewer has to be able to make the questions sound natural and spontaneous.

On the other hand, in order for the answers from one person to be comparable with the answers from another, there must be some way of ensuring that the questions are posed fairly and equally. One could imagine, for example, the same question posed in two quite different ways:

> 'Having seen some pretty awful things in other companies, overall I'd say that our employer treats us pretty well, wouldn't you agree?'

or

> 'All my friends seem to have better employers than me; I guess you'd agree with me that we're treated pretty badly here?'

Obviously the above questions are phrased to be highly leading, and it is hoped that good interviewers would never stoop so low. However, it is easy to decide to alter the way in which a question is put or a topic raised, based on personal feelings at the time, such as whether or not the interviewer supports it or if they feel that the interviewee may have strong feelings on the subject. Even subtle variations such as emphasis can change the way in which a question is perceived and answered, so the interviewer has to maintain a delicate balance between making the conversation appear natural and allowing a different emphasis between interviewers or interviewees.

This can be managed through consultation and practice. The interviewers and programme designers need to meet regularly and often before the first actual interviews start in order to make sure that each person has the same approach and that they can become comfortable enough with the questions to be able to put them naturally and simply without deviating from the original intent.

BASIC RULES

It is beyond my scope to deal with discussion techniques in detail here since this is handled in some detail by other authors. I should say, though, that the familiar basics of conducting a good interview and discussion should apply:

- Keep the questions brief and clear.
- Make it obvious when you have finished and that you expect the other person to speak.
- Allow the interviewee sufficient time to respond.
- Do not answer your own questions.
- Do not suggest answers.
- Be aware of the passage of time.
- Do not be afraid of occasional short silences.

RECORDING ANSWERS

Obviously the answers given are only of use if they are written down. This can be tricky if one of the aims is to create a flowing conversation; flow is interrupted by waiting for somebody to make copious notes. Unfortunately there is not much that can be done about this. The interviewer does have to write down what is said and do it at sufficient length to adequately record the person's feelings and opinions; just giving them a tick on a scale of 1 to 5 reduces it, again, to the level of a survey.

One commonly suggested way of tackling the problem is to record the interviews on tape (or, I suppose, digitally if you possess the technology). This does, of course, remove the need to interrupt the conversation for any writing. The disadvantage that is usually encountered is that it is distracting for the interviewee. People mistrust recording devices simply because it makes them feel self-conscious, or even because they wonder to what use their recording will later be put or perhaps that it might fall into the wrong hands (remember that the interview is supposed to be entirely confidential and anonymous).

The most usual, and probably the best, technique is to create a mixture of flexibility for the interviewer and a set of standard recording formats. I usually take the trouble to create a form listing the questions/topics along one side, with one or two further columns that provide space for me to write something under a number of headings – for example, 'satisfaction', 'complaints', 'desired changes'. This gives me the freedom to conduct an interview in which I am not simply ticking a checklist but at least do not have to spend time writing the topic and headings on a notepad, with the attendant possibility that I may not later be able to interpret what I wrote down. Within the standard format outlined above, each interviewer has the discretion to record each person's answers in a way they see fit – after all, they will later have to be involved in carrying out the analysis.

Answers must be recorded as fully as possible; it may be tempting for the interviewer to make minimal notes in the interests of disrupting the flow of the conversation as little as possible, but this is also likely to provide a minimal level of information. It will be impossible for an interviewer to remember the details of answers to each question in a long interview, or to interpret skimpy notes some time later. This problem is compounded when the interviewer has conducted a number of sessions with the same set of questions, as the answers from one person can easily become confused in memory with those of another. Although it may seem to act as an unnatural break and interfere with the rhythm of the interview, the interviewer must take enough time to note down the details of what is said so that a valid analysis can be undertaken later.

As with other aspects of conducting interviews, the way an interview team can only ensure that the records are made well is through practice and rehearsal. An interviewer needs to be able to 'hit the ground running' at the very first interview and not wait until they have completed a few before becoming good at making notes. By practising a few times and discussing the techniques with the other members of the project and interview teams it should be possible to develop an adequate recording technique.

DEALING WITH DEVIATIONS

Some drift from the agenda is inevitable during some interviews. While many employees will stick strictly to what is asked of them, others may see the interview as a way of getting things off their chests, or may simply be naturally rather garrulous. Again, the policy here is balance. It is certainly not appropriate to allow interviewees to talk at length about their own pet subject since it risks running out of time and draws attention away from the real issues which in turn could lead to poor interpretation of what the person thinks about the important points.

This problem can be relatively easy to deal with if the employee asks whether the interviewer minds if they speak about a particular topic. The first response to this is ask if it is directly relevant to the question that has just been asked. If not, the interviewer response should suggest that the interviewee should wait until later because the topic may be addressed by a later question. If it relates to an earlier question, the additional point should be politely listened to, but if it goes on too long, it is best to politely point out that this topic has already been covered and that it is important to deal with all the intended subjects.

This approach is also appropriate if the interviewee wanders off on to a different subject; simply suggest that there may be an opportunity for them to discuss the matter later as the response to a subsequent question or, perhaps, at the very end. Then, if there is time at the end, the employee should be given the chance to vent their feelings on their chosen topic, as long as the overall time for the interview does not extend dramatically, the reasons for which I have explained earlier in this chapter. If there is not enough time, the interviewer should just firmly say that, unfortunately, time has run out but a great deal of useful information has been gathered already and that, if the person feels strongly enough, perhaps they would like to take up any further topics with their manager.

The most difficult situation to deal with is if the person goes off at a slight tangent but argues that what they are saying does still relate to the question. This is best treated as a time management issue. If the interviewee is expounding upon their pet topic, which has little relevance to the theme of the interview or the subject currently under discussion, it should not be difficult or damaging to merely say that time is limited and there is a lot to get through, and suggest pressing on to the next question.

Remember, though, that deviation is not necessarily a bad thing. Occasionally something may be said that does not relate directly to a particular question or predetermined topic, but is highly pertinent in terms of the overall objective of the interview exercise. The interviewer must be sensitive enough to be able to pick out those few occasions where the deviation is useful, distinguishing it from the inevitable 'waffle' that will arise from time to time. There must also be a place in the analysis and reporting system to allow room for such extra information as this can represent one of the strengths of interviews over other measurement techniques.

ANALYSING THE RESULTS

Producing a meaningful analysis of responses to interviews is far harder than carrying out the same task for survey or continuous monitoring measurement techniques. This is principally because the results are not directly quantifiable but are based on people's articulation of their thoughts, ideas and feelings. There are probably as many ways of approaching this type of analysis as there are managers, since each of us has our own way, formal or otherwise, of interpreting our discussions with staff.

For very small numbers of staff, it should be possible just to sit down and describe the range of things that everybody said in answer to each question and draw conclusions as to what it all means; this can work reasonably well for small populations, especially if there is only one interviewer involved. With significant numbers of interviewees, however, or with multiple interviewers, something more complex needs to be undertaken. Below I describe an approach that seems to work and provides as good a result as I have seen in any such exercises.

STEP 1: CATEGORIZE THE ANSWERS

The first step is to gather all of the interviewers together with the design team (if different) to discuss the answers that were obtained and what they mean. Then for each question and group of questions (since, like the survey questionnaire, questions will undoubtedly be grouped into related sections) the team should come up with a set of categories of answers that have been obtained.

For example, it is possible that a number of people, when asked how satisfied they are with internal general communication, replied that they would like more personal information to be made available, such as the successes or achievements of people outside working hours. Although nobody will have used exactly the same words, it could be that a number have the same overall idea so that this response could be considered to represent a category of answers. These categories will then be listed as responses in the final report.

Determining these categories is usually an iterative process whereby discussions go round the topics until some general agreement emerges as to what they are. Note that this can be very time-consuming. To save time it is also possible for an individual to conduct the exercise alone and then review the outcome with the other interviewers, although I do not usually recommend it since it is often difficult to interpret notes made by others and may even lead to errors through the reviewer missing something important without others to spot the gap.

The outcome of this step is a set of standard responses, similar to those that might be set up at the start of a survey. The differences are that the answers are unlikely to be simply a scale of feelings from 0 to 5 and may possibly be a list of widely varied response categories, and that the list has been created after the fact, based directly on what people have said, rather than a predetermined set of possible responses into which people have to pigeonhole their complex emotions.

STEP 2: ASSIGN ANSWERS TO CATEGORIES

Once the categories have been defined, the group should go back through the answers to each question and assign each one from each respondent to one of the categories. This can be done more successfully by a single analyst than the definition of the categories themselves. Once the categories are known, each interviewer could individually go through their own answer sheets and decide which answer belongs where. In fact interviewers may well find that the group session of creating the category list is difficult enough and, in need of a change of setting, would be happier to perform this task alone. The only reason for undertaking this step as a team effort is if there is some doubt as to how independent and objective the individual allocation would be (although if there is real doubt about this, the interviewers were probably badly chosen in the first place).

Care needs to be taken to ensure that the interview responses are correctly assigned. If, for instance, we have two categories which are 'Salaries here are too low' and 'There are large pay discrepancies in the company' and one response was 'The salaries in technical support are too low; people with the same qualifications in development earn much more' it might be easy to read the first half of the answer and suggest that it belongs in the first category, whereas it probably really sits better in the second.

The exact wording or details of the responses should be retained for future reference and more detailed study. It is not enough, when subsequently determining a precise course of action, to simply know how many people gave a response in a certain category; that would result in a loss of much of the information gained.

STEP 3: DEFINE THE STRENGTH OF THE RESPONSES

Although the last thing that I said under step 2 was that the detail of each response should not be discarded, it will also be useful to have some general, quantifiable information in the final report against each category. In order to provide this alongside the detail, the interview team need to determine the strength of feeling in each response. When suggesting that salaries are too low, for example, one person might say 'Well, I could do with a little more, but it's not too bad' whereas another may say 'It's disgusting. Most of the men I work with struggle to do more than just feed their families on what this place pays'. Clearly there is a different level of feeling in these two answers.

The strength of each response, then, should therefore be considered and graded, perhaps on a scale of 0 to 5 or 0 to 10, in a similar manner to that used for scoring survey responses. Just as with surveys, every person's opinions should be taken into account, even if they have nothing to say on the subject, in which case they should be given a 'zero'. The analysts should also discuss the definition of what each score means before the grading takes place, in order to ensure consistency of scoring between the interviewers and individual responses (interviewers normally carry out this grading exercise themselves since it is impractical for the whole team to do it except for very small interview populations).

> **TIP**
> The interview will have to have been managed and recorded in such a way that every topic is brought up at some point, so that each respondent is at least given the chance to comment on it, otherwise this scoring method will have less meaning.

The overall strength of response in each category is then calculated by taking the mean of all scores. This is done to show managers where overall feeling is strongest and allows those response categories created by extreme comments by just one or two individuals to be filtered out; if there is a small number of high scores but most are zero or very low, then the score in this category will show that it is less of an issue than one arousing reasonably strong feelings among a large proportion of the workforce, despite the possibly striking comments that appear in the detail of the responses. Just as with other measurements, looking at the range or spread of measurements and reporting these alongside the mean will also be of some benefit, since it will indicate the homogeneity of the workforce's feelings. A large spread of responses in terms of salary, for example, will show that it is only a few that are unhappy with pay levels.

STEP 4: DRAW OVERALL CONCLUSIONS

Once we have allocated and scored all responses, it is time for the project team to get together once more to discuss what overall conclusions should be drawn from the analysis. Although the managers for whom the report is intended are likely to be quite capable of making up their own minds about things, the output of an interview programme of any size is likely to be highly complex. The people who have been involved in running the programme will be in a far better position to understand that complexity than a manager who is seeing it for the first time. The project team therefore needs to prepare a set of pointers to where the most interesting and useful information lies and what it means.

There is no special technique or standard method for this. It simply requires a review of the data available and the application of some professional judgement as to what it represents. Generally, I try to avoid, at this stage, simply pointing out where the category scores are highest, because this is obvious. I would use these simply as an indicator of where to start my study and then try to look at the actual responses themselves, aiming to pull out those areas of particular interest and perhaps also attempting to consider the underlying reason for those responses. For example, job insecurity may well manifest itself in a variety of small concerns about other issues such as pay, terms and conditions, communication and so on.

Drawing conclusions must be a group activity. One person – the project leader, for example – working alone may well miss important clues or could apply a personal slant to the interpretation of the results. Having the whole team conduct the discussion and drawing out the major conclusions is more likely to produce a complete and fair analysis.

STEP 5: PREPARE THE REPORT

With all of this information, the final output from the project team should be a written report to those in the organization responsible for taking action – the people who wanted the exercise carried out in the first place (the 'clients'). The purpose of the report is to present the findings of the interview programme in a way that allows those not involved in the design or interviews to understand what information was gained and what it means, permitting them to make decisions about future actions. As such, I usually prefer that the report of the programme does not include recommendations, although if the project's clients wish the project team to make recommendations this can always be provided as a separate document. The reason why I prefer to keep them separate is to try to maintain the purity and usefulness of the information gained. If the report contains recommendations there is a high risk that subsequent debate will centre on whether or not to accept the recommendations and not on the nature of the findings.

Report structure

The report should, of course, follow the accepted rules for good written reports with a clear layout, introductions, background, references and so on. The body of the report should contain three sections:

- For each question group, *the strength of response to each answer category*, shown both in graphical and tabular form, as illustrated in Figure 7.1 and Table 7.1. If the overall number of questions was not too large, it may also be possible to do this for each individual topic; although this is highly desirable because some information is lost when grouping questions, it could be impractical if the volume of data is too large. When there is too much information to present it all, the project team may elect to include in the report results for those topics which appear to produce the most interesting results.
- *A description, analysis and discussion of each answer category* for each question group. Again, this may be extended to cover individual topics using the same criteria as for the numerical data.
- *The overall conclusions.*

Even by only using question groups and the occasional individual topic, the volume of data presented in the report is likely to be large. Some of the usual tricks to make this manageable should be employed as far as possible, such as providing summaries in the main report and keeping much of the detail as appendices. In this way, the project team can cater not only for those who are not interested in the detail but might be willing to read the summaries, but also for those to whom the detail is all-

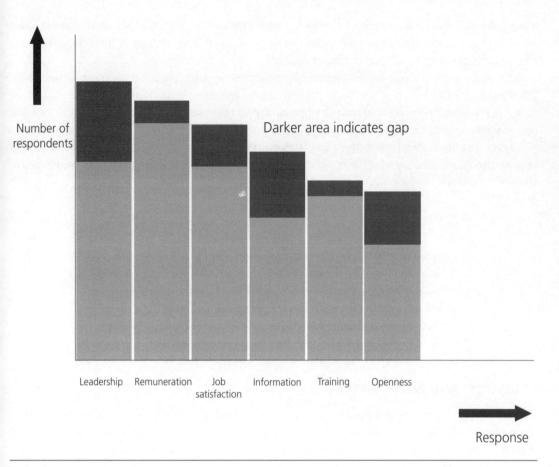

Figure 7.1 Interview response chart

Table 7.1 Report of interview data

Topic	Mean importance	Mean current situation	Gap of means
Leadership	8.9	6.3	2.6
Remuneration	8.3	7.8	0.5
Job satisfaction	8.1	7.1	1.0
Availability of information	7.4	5.2	2.2
Training and development	6.9	6.7	0.2
Openness and fairness	6.8	5.1	1.7

important and will not take the report seriously without it. Bear in mind that it will even be necessary to prepare all the raw data from the interview programme – actual individual responses, for example – in a way that can be presented and studied by others just in case some data-hungry executive demands it. Do not, however, automatically present such data to each report recipient since it will deter many of them from even reading the summary.

It is a good idea to try the report out before circulating it to its final audience. Certainly the whole project team should have a chance to comment on it, but perhaps a friendly executive could also give it some thought (the project client 'champion', if such a person has been nominated, would be a good choice). This can save embarrassment at having to re-release the report later if there are some areas where a change in analysis or presentation is needed.

Ideally, the report should be first viewed by its principal target audience at a project presentation. The managers with an interest or stake in the final results should be invited to a meeting where the key points of the report are presented with an opportunity for questions and verbal explanation. This can be especially important where the volume of data in the report is large, since it will both help managers to understand it better and reduce the number of subsequent questions and misinterpretations. At the end of the presentation, bound copies can then be given to the attendees to study at their leisure.

> TIP
>
> I prefer to give reports out at the end because it encourages the audience to listen to the presentation rather than read an unrelated section of the report while I am speaking, but I know that some people would rather give the report out at the beginning so that the audience can refer to what is being said on the page in front of them. The choice is yours, but try to think about what you want to do and why.

STRENGTHS AND WEAKNESSES

The use of interviews to measure people within the organization can be a powerful and effective tool. It has many strengths both in its own right and in comparison with the other two major techniques that I have described in this book. It also has some drawbacks, however, and I have ended this chapter with some thoughts on what those strengths and weaknesses are.

STRENGTHS

- One of the biggest positive points for using an interview to measure is that it gives direct access to the real, freely-voiced thoughts of individuals.
- Although the interview is usually structured around a limited set of questions, it gives people the opportunity to say what they like about any subject they like.
- It makes people feel more personally involved in the process.
- It allows for interpretation of actual feedback from interviewees and not just numbers on a sliding scale.
- There is maximum opportunity for dealing with highly specific issues that arise from small groups.

WEAKNESSES

- It is far more time-consuming and disruptive than the other two techniques.
- Finding impartial and trusted interviewers can be difficult and the use of external experts is often required.
- The results and analysis rely heavily on personal interpretation of what was said.
- It is difficult to compare answers from one person with those of another.
- It is much harder to use a 100 per cent sample of employees than with the questionnaire survey.

- Since interviews can only be conducted one at a time it is likely that there will be significant elapsed time between the first interview in the cycle and the last one.
- Although there needs to be flexibility, a standard set of questions should be defined as part of the design process.
- The ways in which questions are put should be as standard as possible between interviews.
- Questions should follow a defined structure and should never be put in a leading or misleading way.
- The venue for the interview should be away from the normal workplace, private and free of distractions.
- A simple, yet standard, way of recording answers needs to be defined to ensure the reliability of subsequent analysis.

SUMMARY

- The interview technique is used to gain more impressions and information than can be garnered from paper questionnaires.
- Interviews are often conducted by independent and impartial external experts.
- This type of measurement programme has very high visibility.
- Careful design, planning and scheduling is necessary to make an interview scheme work well.
- Timing is especially important, both in terms of time allowed for the interview and completing them all within a defined period.
- The interviewer needs to be able to allow freedom to express feelings and ideas without permitting the interview to lose its focus.
- Analysis comprises answer categorization, allocation to categories, determining the strength of responses, drawing conclusions from the results and the preparation of a report.
- The technique has strengths and weaknesses that make interviews right in some circumstances but inappropriate in others.

CHAPTER EIGHT

Monitoring People

THE CONTINUOUS MEASUREMENT TECHNIQUE

The third method of measuring people is by finding ways of continually watching signs and signals in order to form conclusions about how people are both feeling and performing. This 'stand-back-and-watch' approach is far less intrusive than either the survey or interview techniques. It is also a scheme that can provide a regular or continuous stream of data rather than the single-shot feedback that comes from surveys and interviews.

However, perhaps the principal difference between this and the other two techniques described in this book is that it tends to measure behaviour, whereas the others measure feelings and opinions. Where a questionnaire or interview might, for example, find out whether or not employees consider the main noticeboard to be interesting and of value, direct monitoring would identify how often they actually go to it and read what is there.

PROS AND CONS

As can be expected, because it has these different characteristics, the technique of monitoring of daily work has both advantages and disadvantages over the other two methods.

Advantages

The biggest benefit of continuous monitoring is simply that it is continuous. Surveys and interviews are intended to be snapshots, conducted within a short space of time and analysed to produce a picture of what was happening at the time they were conducted. They represent an image of what was going on during the project period and say little about the situation before or after. They cannot be conducted too often since they are costly, time-consuming and intrusive so their use needs to be restricted to, say, once a year. A scheme that monitors signs and signals, on the other hand, can provide daily results if necessary and appropriate.

Another key point is that it can be introduced gradually, starting with one or two simple indicators and then growing. The one-shot nature of surveys and interviews means that they need to be conducted again if further topics are to be added, and it is often not worth conducting them just for a small issue. Continuous monitoring, though, can be used as narrowly or broadly as required.

As I mentioned above, it is the least intrusive of the three methods. Although it should always be done with the knowledge and acceptance of the workforce (since, otherwise, it is more like spying than managing), at the routine level people need hardly be aware that a measurement is actually being taken. This contrasts with the time and disruption caused by the two questioning techniques – particularly the interview approach.

The fact that behaviours are measured can also be seen as an advantage. After all, what is important for the results of the organization (in most cases) is what people do, not what their opinions are.

Disadvantages

The main disadvantage of this technique, when compared to the other two, is simply that it is more difficult. Surveys are probably the most common form of employee measurement because they are not that difficult to create and manage. At the simplest level, we do nothing more than throw together a few questions on a sheet of paper, give a range of responses from low to high, mark them as 1 to 5 and just report the mean averages of the results. Obviously, there are better surveys that require more intellectual effort, but the basic form is neither difficult to carry out nor to conceptualize. Almost any manager in an organization could probably run a survey if they needed to.

Remote monitoring, on the other hand, is more tricky. A manager asked to set up such a programme may well not know where to begin. What to monitor, how to turn observations into a measurement of something that we wish to understand and how to interpret what we see require careful thought and application.

Another drawback is that the results may be less immediately acceptable to the workforce. Since people feel that they have directly contributed to a survey or interview programme, they can see that what comes out relates to what they have put in. With independent monitoring, however, they may feel that they have had no control over how the monitoring is done or interpreted and may distrust the output. This can only be overcome with careful planning and programme design, coupled with excellent internal communications.

Probably the third most significant pitfall relates to the staying power of managers. Because surveys and interviews are highly visible and relatively self-contained, there is a strong driving force to complete the programme and publish the results. Continuous monitoring is, of course, continuous. This means that it is a constant, ongoing task that regularly occupies management and staff time. As a result, a measurement initiative of this type can often fail because people lose their initial enthusiasm and become bored with it, or simply because it receives a lower priority than some other tasks or projects and is dropped during busy or pressurized periods. This can be largely avoided by making it a central part of management strategy and something that is demanded by the organization's leaders alongside more traditional information; this comes back to the all-important need for commitment and enthusiasm for measuring at the very top of the organization's structure.

Finally, I have to list the fact that this technique measures behaviours as a potential disadvantage, even though it has already been described as an advantage. This is because measuring often affects the way in which people behave, they may unconsciously behave differently while they are being monitored to those occasions when they are not; by contrast, surveys and interviews may give a truer picture if conditions are created to encourage people to be honest.

OVERALL MEASUREMENT LINKAGE

The continuous monitoring approach is also much closer to other types of measurement than surveys and interviews. Most business measurements, such as product characteristics, financial status, sales figures and so on, are reported at regular intervals based on either entire sets of data or on some form of regular sampling.

This means that the monitoring style of people measurement can be integrated with other measurement systems. Once the methods and collection techniques have been established, they can be applied and reported together with other business measurements to provide a comprehensive corporate picture and to allow for correlation between different operational and situational characteristics.

DESIGNING THE SYSTEM

As with any other programme of this nature, spending time on getting the design right is essential for a successful final result. Many of the first steps are similar to defining the question topics for interviews and surveys. Since, however, the flavour is slightly different, I explain the entire process below from the first steps.

WHAT TO MEASURE

Our first task is to determine what we would like to be able to measure in general, before we leap into defining exactly what we wish to monitor. This is vital if we are to avoid the pitfall of picking something that we can easily measure rather than something that is really meaningful. For example, it would be easy to measure how many people turn up for organized social events, but attendance could be more to do with employees' social preferences or domestic commitments than an indicator of how much they feel part of the company 'family'.

Review objectives

The very first thing to do, then, is to review the overall objectives of the organization. If the company does not have any, or they are out-of-date, or exist only in the CEO's head, some work will need to be done to define them in a way that leads to common understanding.

From the overall objectives, we should consider what characteristics of the workforce are desirable (or positively undesirable) and will have an immediate impact on the objectives. Sometimes it may also be necessary to define a second level – that is, what behaviours or attitudes contribute towards the main characteristics. For example, we may state that we want our employees to be committed to customer satisfaction; however, this is such a large and imprecise characteristic that we may then feel that we need to define those things that lead to customer satisfaction, or demonstrate commitment. These could include willingness to deal with a customer problem at the end of the working day, helpfulness to customers even when it is not really that particular employee's job, or even how much your staff grumble about customer requests. From there, we can proceed to identify specific measurables.

Determine measurable characteristics

Once we have the list of employee characteristics, it needs to be studied to determine which of them we have some idea of how to measure. I used to feel, at this point in defining such a programme, that one should also decide over which aspects any influence can be brought to bear and ignore those where it could not. For example, it may be desirable for employees to have an enjoyable and varied set of outside interests but, since these have nothing to do with their employment, they should be left out of any measurement programme.

I have, however, now changed my mind. If what we want is information that enables us to both monitor our workforce and act as input to our decision-making, then all information is valuable. There may well be things that we have no control over yet will influence other decisions that we wish to make. As an example, let us look at the analogy of taking a journey by car. We cannot control factors such as traffic, weather conditions or roadworks (although I am hoping that science will one day advance to the point where the mysteries of roadworks are understood and can be inoculated against) but these factors will nevertheless influence our setting off time, the route that we take and even whether to undertake the journey at all. Similarly, there may be several signs that people might reveal through measurement that have an impact on what we do. For instance, if it is discovered that many employees are worried about an impending economic recession, it might be a good time to display more financial openness and show people how good the company's short- and long-term prospects are.

We usually use common sense to determine the characteristics that are measurable – that is, we simply look at the list that has been generated and tick those that we can readily measure. This task is best undertaken in a group of three to six project team members, working in a brainstorming and problem-solving mode. The group meets in a place where they will not be disturbed for a while, spends a little time 'warming up', then goes down the list tackling each item in turn. It is important that each one is properly considered, allowing enough time to be sure whether it can be measured or not. Usually the best technique is not to ask 'Can we measure this one?' but to have a facilitator who says 'Let's have ideas on how to measure this one'.

I like to apply brainstorming rules to such sessions, in that ideas should be taken at face value and without judgement or criticism as they are first put forward, until the idea stream is exhausted, and only then permitting evaluation of the merits of each.

Often it will be discovered that the item on the list cannot be measured directly, but somebody will come up with an idea of how we can measure something similar. There is nothing wrong with this, and such suggestions can provide unexpected excellent measurements that would not have come to light using a more straightforward approach.

Match measurable characteristics to objectives

The final step in deciding what to measure is to take the list of measurable characteristics and compare them to the organization's objectives. The first pass should simply try to assign the measurement to one or more objectives; if such an assignment cannot be made (that is, it does not seem to relate to an objective), the measurement area should removed from the list for consideration since it is not particularly relevant to our overall aims. This provides an initial filter for what might be a very long list.

In some cases, this process may result in a list of measurable items that seems just the right length for a practical measurement programme – enough items to ensure that the measurements are not too narrowly focused but not so many that the programme becomes unmanageable. It is also possible, however, that the list will still be too long. If so, a good approach is to assign scores to each measurement to indicate how well it measures achievement of, or progress towards, objectives. If an item applies to more than one objective, it benefits from having two or more scores, which should be added to produce a final value. Then it is a simple process to make a group decision as to how many items can practically be monitored and pick the highest scoring ones from the remaining list.

This is, of course, an iterative process. Scoring and other artificial ranking techniques are only a tool and their results should not be applied blindly. The top scoring set should be reviewed to ensure that it makes sense, that some important items have not accidentally been omitted and that it is of the right length. User and functional groups within the organization should probably also be consulted at this stage. This will result in a final, agreed list of measurement items that can be implemented. In fact, the final choice of measurements may well reflect what happens when we toss a coin to make a decision – if the coin lands a certain way up we are disappointed, which reveals to us the decision that we really wanted to make.

> **TIP**
>
> Do not assume, just because you have decided that you can comfortably measure 20 items, that the final list must contain exactly 20. If you have 19 and are scratching around for one more, then perhaps you should leave it there. Alternatively do not exclude number 21 if it is just as good a measurement as number 20.

PLANNING AND PREPARATION

We have all heard the old adage that 'he who fails to plan, plans to fail'. This is just as true of measurements by monitoring as for any other business activity. It might be tempting to simply give the list of measurable characteristics to managers and tell them to get on with it, but doing so would not produce the best results. A more professional approach is to first consider the who, where, when and how we will measure before we begin.

RESPONSIBILITY

Before anything can be done, it has to be known who will do it. Unlike the other two types of measurement that I have already described, continuous monitoring does not require a coherent project team – first, because it is not a project since it has no natural end point but is regular and ongoing and, second, because the measurements may well be centred around a specific group or area. For example, most of the measurements related to the canteen are best taken by the canteen manager or one of the canteen staff. Thus most measurements will fall naturally into the area of responsibility of one or two people, and it is most logical for the remit to take and conduct the initial analysis of measurements to be allocated to them.

So, the people who will take the measurements and make sense of them will have to be identified (these are not necessarily, of course, the people who will later initiate action). Once they have been appointed, the design process can continue to involve them at every stage so that they can identify what is practical and suggest how any proposed changes would operate within their own area of expertise.

> **TIP**
>
> Even though an overall coordinating project team is not required, it might be a good idea to create a small group that meets occasionally to review the operation of the measurement programme and ensure that it stays fresh and lively.

SAMPLING

The next step is to determine how the data will be sampled. The usual first choice in a measurement programme is to decide whether to sample at all, or whether to count every piece of data available. Sampling is common in many industries – for example, a factory might decide to measure the size of a component by measuring every one produced, or could decide that some representative sample would suffice, say by checking one in every ten. Engineers and others with a penchant for technical and numerical accuracy might employ a standard such as BS 6001 or ISO 2589 to determine how many samples they should measure in order to gain their desired level of confidence in their results.

When considering people measurements, two things come to mind:

- We will inevitably have to conduct some form of sampling since we cannot gauge every reaction of every person every time that it occurs.
- The level of sampling will have to be derived naturally, since applying statistical rigour to such things is precarious because we do not have a narrowly defined sample and measurement size.

Let us look at a measurement of something that is as typically difficult to monitor as adherence to the company culture: employees' dedication to customer satisfaction. It is possible it is determined that one way in which this can be measured is by how often an employee will stay late to resolve a customer question or problem, rather than tell the customer that it will be dealt with tomorrow. A supervisor trying to monitor this will probably try to capture every time that one or the other occurs, but this will rely on the supervisor knowing about it somehow, which in some environments could be very difficult. Thus, the only instances noticed will be those that are recorded. This is a form of sampling imposed by the restrictions of measuring people-based phenomena. Similarly, it is impossible to say that the details (for example, the length of time worked late) will only be recorded every third occasion since we will not know when every third event occurs.

However there are still some deliberations to be made here. We may, for instance, decide to sample by restricting ourselves to a group or selection of employees, because trying to measure them all is impractical. Or we might decide to measure only for a limited period per year, because continuous monitoring represents too great an administrative burden. Whatever the final decision, it must be considered as part of the design phase because it has implications for how the data will be taken and used.

FREQUENCY

Part of the decision about sampling will be to determine how often measurements should be taken. Should they be taken every time that a particular event occurs, or daily, or monthly?

Perhaps, for instance, we wish to monitor how soon people leave the premises at the end of the working day to identify the extent of 'clock watching'; those who leave within two or three minutes must have stopped working before the end of their day in order to hit the door so early. We have a choice of how to measure this; we could use records from a clocking/punching out system to note each person's times for every day or shift, which would be possible if such a system were strictly used. Alternatively, we could stand by the door and make notes; this would be tiresome on a daily basis so we may decide to do it just once per week (shifting the day of sampling each week so that we do not get a picture biased by the behaviours on a certain day). Our prior decisions on sampling would also affect what proportion of the workforce we would study in this way; frequency and sample size are inextricably interlinked since they have a direct impact on the total volume of data produced.

Decisions on measurement frequency are usually influenced largely by practical considerations. First, we cannot measure something more often than it actually occurs. Second, if the event occurs too often, it not only may not be possible to witness it every time, but it may also produce too much data to sensibly analyse and quantify. There is also the simple practical point, already mentioned above, that we may not witness every occurrence. A supervisor may wish to measure the number of the times that a request for assistance is received from another department and how often it is answered positively and how often refused or accepted reluctantly; however, they can only record the event if they actually see it – if they are away from their desk they may not even know that it has happened. In such cases, the decision on frequency may be just to note it every time that it is seen, knowing that not every occurrence will be witnessed.

METHOD

Another key decision that must be made about the measurement before any data can be gathered is exactly how we will obtain the information. In many cases, the answer to this is obvious – for example, finding out how many 'hits' occur in the news section of our intranet service is simply a matter of defining a counter for the appropriate page. On the other hand, even something as straightforward as noting the attendance at lunchtime briefing sessions (which could measure both the interest and motivation of employees and the effectiveness of the sessions themselves) needs a decision – do we count heads at the door, ask them to sign an attendance sheet, do an informal count while the briefer is speaking, or even ask a selection of employees on a regular basis to let us know how many briefing sessions they have attended during the month?

Table 8.1 Measurement method examples

Measured item	Method employed
Interest in reading corporate news bulletins	Number of 'hits' on the news intranet site, counted automatically
Interest in the corporate community	Number of independent contributions to the site newsletter, logged on receipt by the editorial team via a tally chart
Belief in health and safety	Number of health and safety risks reported, logged by the H&S adviser as part of the reporting and analysis system
Eagerness for improvement	Number of suggestions made via the suggestion scheme, counted daily by the HR officer
Attention to visitors	Number of unattended people seen wearing visitor badges, noted on a tally sheet in a notebook by the works manager, noted as he sees them when walking about
Satisfaction with their job	Number of accesses per week to known Internet recruitment sites, measured automatically by the IT system, with the known job site list updated monthly by the IT manager
Whether the amount of time on distributing jokes is within reasonable limits	Number of e-mails sent to purpose-made 'jokes' group on the company e-mail system, measured automatically
Care taken of company property	Frequency of requests for replacement protective equipment, uniforms and so on, measured by adding to a tally chart every time that a request form is handed in
Attention to data security	A daily walk around the office to determine how many people have left their desks without engaging the password protection lock
Eagerness for personal development	Attendance at lunchtime training and information sessions, measured by counting the numbers on the attendance sheets
Work pressure	Average number of hours worked beyond standard hours, measured by a weekly report from the timekeeping security entrance system

In some cases, difficulty over deciding how to collect the data can reveal that we have selected an unrealistic measurement. We might, for instance, decide that we wish to measure loyalty by counting the number of times that employees support official policy against those occasions when they specifically decry it. The problem here is that there is simply no way of noting each and every occurrence of support or otherwise. The people responsible for spotting such things may well pick up a few occasions, but there will be many opinions that are simply not noticed or will be expressed out of earshot of the measurers so that any occurrences that we do note cannot be placed in context of the wider picture. Indeed, what paltry measurement we could make will be distorted by the fact that statements made publicly are likely to be far more loyal than those made privately. This is, then, an impractical measurement and we need to find something simpler to monitor. Indeed, it is an illustration of the general inability of this type of measurement to identify opinions; if we wish to identify such things, then it would be better to use a questionnaire.

It is important to choose a method that is practical and reliable. It must be an exercise that can easily be carried out, yields readily accessible data and is not too onerous. An exercise that is very difficult to implement will quickly be dropped or forgotten, and the desired measurement will either be unavailable or meaningless. Examples of some of the methods that I have seen used are given in Table 8.1.

RECORDING AND REPORTING

A crucial part of defining the method of data collection should also be to create a standard way of recording the information gained, since the information has to be in a format compatible with other sets of data once the time arrives for analysis. For example, a manager may elect to measure the effectiveness of monthly departmental meetings by picking two people after each meeting, asking them how they thought it went and judging their reactions; when analysed, this data will be fairly useless if on one occasion the reactions were scaled against a predefined list, at another time they were described longhand and at yet another they were ranked from 1 to 5 on a 'goodness' scale. Similarly, the data are only useful if they are complete; if we judge the meetings by an end-of-meeting questionnaire, then data showing that 20 per cent of people thought the meeting was too long one month and 50 per cent thought so the following month is meaningless if we do not know how many people attended each event. (For example, if there were ten people at the first meeting and only four at the second, it could have been the same two people who always think that all meetings go on too long.)

One solution is to create some type of standard reporting form, spreadsheet or database, so that it is clear what information has to be recorded each time. Then the person making the recording is guided to record the details in a particular fashion.

In fact, for all this type of monitoring I prefer to use forms over training, written procedures and so on. We can record data on any old scrap piece of paper, but using a form reminds us what information to take, what format it should be in, how it should be structured and so on. If we find that half the form is empty, then (provided that the form has been well designed) we have probably not taken sufficient data; if we find that there is nowhere to write down some snippet, we should conclude that this particular piece of information is not required.

COMMUNICATION

Communication with the measurement team and with the workforce at large is a key requirement of the planning and preparation stage. Obviously the team must know what the programme is about, when it will start, how it will work and what their roles are. This should also extend beyond the tasks assigned to each individual – the whole team should be kept aware of the whole picture so that they can see their place within it and understand the context of their own activities.

It is perhaps more important, though, for the whole workforce to be kept informed. People need to be told that they are being monitored, what the purpose of that monitoring is and what will be done with the results. I suppose, theoretically, it could be possible to perform some sort of undercover surveillance of the workforce without their knowledge, but in most cases some inkling of what was happening would inevitably creep out, lending to widespread suspicion, wariness and resentment. Making everybody totally aware of what is happening eliminates fear and misunderstanding. Moreover, the knowledge that certain aspects of their work are being monitored is likely to make people more diligent in those areas being measured.

TAKING THE MEASUREMENTS

In theory the actual taking of the measurements should be a simple task since the whole system will have been adequately designed, planned and communicated in advance so that there is nothing left undecided or uncertain. This includes who collects the data, how often, from what size sample, how it is recorded, how what is seen is interpreted and to whom or where the data are sent for analysis.

There are two especially important things to remember when the project has progressed to the taking of measurements:

● Data must be gathered when required – gaps in the data set will reduce the value of the measurements and, in some cases, will render them worthless.
● Data must be collected in the prescribed manner and at the prescribed time. Data that are not compatible with the overall set can be worse than data that are missing since it could lead to misleading results, with the potential consequences of erroneous analysis and inappropriate action.

It is a good idea if those taking the measurements also take care to create the right balance of local awareness. As I have already emphasized, it is important that the people being measured understand what is going on and why. Therefore no data collection should be done surreptitiously or in a manner that is in any way underhand. If somebody asks whether the data collector is measuring them, the answer should be truthful. On the other hand, monitoring does not need to be, to use a modern colloquialism, 'in your face'. The best results with the least disruption are achieved by carrying out the exercise unobtrusively but without secrecy. Even if those being monitored do not feel upset or uncomfortable when being directly measured, the very fact that they are aware of being studied will affect their behaviour and thus the final results.

ANALYSIS

Analysis is dealt with in more detail in Chapter Nine. With particular reference to continuous monitoring, though, we should remember that the method and style of analysis should reinforce the strengths of the measurement method. Since one particular strength of continuous monitoring is its immediacy, analysis should also be carried out in a direct and immediate fashion.

This means, first, that the raw data should be reported so that they indicate exactly what has been looked at and where. Whilst there is no reason not to also include the measurements in some broader evaluation, the fact that we have made direct measurements of our people implies that the results should be available to be called upon when necessary to ensure that nothing is hidden or under-hand.

Second, the basic analysis should be available immediately. Although it is true for all measurements that the more current they are the better, it is particularly important that direct monitoring results are made available straightaway. Apart from the fact that this allows much more timely understanding of a situation than by other methods (a survey usually indicates a person's consistent feelings on a topic, whereas monitoring can identify the momentary response), we also have to remember that those being monitored could become suspicious if the results take a long time to become available.

However, this is not to say that directly monitored parameters necessarily have to be immediately published. In some cases, little will be gained by the early publication of a single measurement that is designed to be combined with others to produce the desired information. The data does, however, need to be made available for review and consultation if requested. And if there is to be amalgamation or calculation, this should be carried out as quickly as possible to retain the immediacy of the results.

REPORTING

TIMELINESS

Timeliness is also one of the prime requirements for reporting. This stems directly from the need for analysis to be direct and immediate; there is little benefit to be gained if we analyse information as soon as it is available but then delay communication until the data no longer has any value. Reporting must be arranged to be sufficiently easy and quick so that information is publicly available as soon as the raw numbers have been analysed.

OPENNESS

Another factor to bear in mind is that this type of measurement, unlike the interview and the survey, may attempt to study what is going on without the direct knowledge or conscious input of the people being measured. Thus, it is likely to be even more important for the reporting mechanism, and the reports themselves, to be open and accessible to everybody. If I have been surveyed, I know how I responded to each point, and the most interesting part of any consequent report will be geared towards telling me how what I said relates to what other people said. If I have been independently monitored, however, I do not really know what my input was since I do not know exactly what the researcher saw and how it was interpreted. I will be less likely to trust the data if the reports are not made clear, open and readily accessible.

This has the obvious implication that the data reports should be made available to everybody. There must be some form of report, made available widely and quickly after the data collection, that can be seen by everybody and that genuinely reflects the way in which the data is being interpreted. This does not stop the measurement team from also producing other reports that provide more sophisticated analyses and offering other reports that show the data both in more and less refined ways – but there must be something that everybody also sees. However, this is not a licence to produce something for the masses to keep them happy while creating something entirely different for the eyes of the 'Politburo' only. Deception is not likely to fulfil the aims of the measurement programme in the long term.

> **TIP**
> It is always a good idea to ensure that copies of any more sophisticated or detailed reports are held as available on request, or even to actively encourage certain people, such as official employee representatives, to seek access to such reports to demonstrate that there is no secrecy or duplicity involved.

CLARITY AND EXPLANATION

There are also other reporting considerations. If we acknowledge that people will need to know what is being said about them, then we must not only issue reports regularly and quickly but must also make sure that they know what the reports mean. Consequently, reports have to be simple, straightforward and easy for everybody to understand, with little opportunity for ambiguity or misunderstanding. This is not a bad thing, since it forces the project team to find ways of analysing and presenting the results of measurements clearly and simply, without overcomplicating and confusing the picture.

The paramount consideration must be to show what is being measured, why, and how the results have been interpreted. It is easy for people to misunderstand or 'get the wrong end of the stick' if measurements and results are not clearly explained. Let us consider the example of a company where data security is of particular importance. They may choose to monitor screen locking, as mentioned earlier, and combine this as a group of measurements with a few others such as:

- using a mystery telephone caller who asks for information without adequate authorization and contrary to company policy
- asking managers, at planned intervals, to approach somebody and ask for confidential data that is not within their sphere of authority
- conducting random security searches on employees leaving the premises to determine whether they have, for example, inadvertently left something that is not supposed to leave the building in their briefcase.

If it becomes apparent that these techniques are being used, people could easily come to believe that there is some form of 'big brother' secret activity going on that is trying to catch people out and make trouble for them, when the purpose of the exercise is to determine the overall state of affairs and not to penalize individuals.

Of course, some will argue that some of the above examples *should* be kept secret, since the 'mystery shopper' approach is more effective if nobody knows about it. Certainly, nobody should know whether the conversation or activity is real or part of a measurement, but knowing that the exercise exists is not nearly as harmful as suspecting that it does but finding that its purpose and findings are shrouded in secrecy. Managers of hotels in large chains, for instance, are well aware that head office will send a mystery guest every now and then, but as they do not know who it will be they cannot tailor their service just for the mystery guest. In fact, knowing that such an inspection may occur keeps people on their toes – as I have already suggested, the very act of measuring can itself improve performance.

AVOIDING INDIVIDUAL DATA

Although people may be interested to see these measurements in order to understand how their behaviour is interpreted, the fact that they are published for access by anybody means that details interpreted from the behaviour of any one single individual should not be presented to avoid potential recriminations or embarrassment. The public data should be reported globally to ensure that they are seen as being of general origin rather than attributable to any one person. Similarly, it must be made clear that there is no blame or anger attached to these results. They must be seen as areas of interest for managers to act upon to improve their systems and culture, never as an excuse to berate an individual or group. Employees will totally lose faith in the process if they believe that what they do and say are interpreted independently as things which later come back and bite them. They should accept the monitoring, though, if they believe that the information will be used for systemic and cultural improvements rather than as an excuse to wield the big stick.

REVIEWING THE SYSTEM

Essential to this type of measurement is that the approach is, and remains, valid and appropriate. In order to achieve this, the system should be constantly reviewed to identify where it could be improved or modified. This is especially important in the early days; it is highly likely that the initial design of each measurement, together with how it will be collected and analysed, will require correction and improvement before it can be considered acceptable. The team must recognize this early on. In recognition of the fact that trust and acceptance is key to the success of continuous monitoring, any review of each measurement must be prompt and public in order to demonstrate that the measurement team is keen to get it right and not continue with something that is not as good as it could be.

It follows that review should include the input of those being measured. They should be given the opportunity to check the results of the measurements against their own fundamental understanding of the nature of things, and a suitable response taken to adjust the measurement techniques and processes where necessary. This does not mean that things should automatically be changed just because those being surveyed are surprised by the results – often the results will tell us something new (indeed, if they never did, the exercise would only have limited value). People being monitored may also have reasons why they do not like measurements being reported; they could show them in a bad light perhaps, or indicate that a change is necessary when they would prefer to maintain the status quo. On the other hand, if the results indicate something that the workforce feel to be wrong, some investigation is certainly needed to verify the validity of the measurement mechanism.

SUMMARY

- Continuous monitoring is about identifying regular signals that tell us how people are behaving.
- The advantages are that it is continuous, can be managed gradually and it is not especially intrusive.
- Disadvantages include complexity and difficulty, poor workforce acceptability and the length of time and effort needed.
- Designing the programme well is vital for success.
- Design of measurements should be carefully linked to corporate and local objectives.
- Planning the programme's introduction is also important.
- Planning must involve identifying frequency and sample sizes, allocating responsibility and ensuring that the plan is well communicated.
- Collection of the data needs to be as unobtrusive as possible to avoid affecting the measurements.

- On the other hand, there should be no secrecy or underhand methods.
- Analysis must be planned in such a way as to maximize consistency.
- Reports may need to be prepared at several levels.
- Reports should be immediate and well explained.
- Reports should not reveal data related to any single person.
- The programme will need to be regularly reviewed for adequacy.

CHAPTER NINE

Analysis and Action

INTRODUCTION

The whole purpose of a measurement regime of any form is to provide information that will guide future actions. It is all very well to have reports that represent in the best possible fashion the way in which people react and behave, but this is only useful if somebody then considers what the reports mean and what they should do about it. Appreciating the when, what and how of actions is not a precise science and will often depend on the nature of the factor being measured. There are, however, a variety of tools and concepts that should be understood and applied as the need arises.

ANALYSIS PERSONNEL

REVIEW TEAM

There are a number of ways in which successful measurement programme reports have been, and can be, reviewed. They can be done at quarterly meetings, in ad hoc groups, by individuals or even by external consultants or specialists. Each has their own merits and disadvantages.

Using a fixed team has the benefit of bringing together a variety of inputs, ideas and specializations that can be brought to bear on any particular set of results. The team needs to be carefully selected so that it incorporates people who are committed to the programme and can provide an adequately wide range of viewpoints; there is little point in having every member of the review team selected from the human resources department.

An ideal team size is from three to six people. They should be from a wide range of disciplines and should have some direct involvement with the design and operation of the programme, the principles behind the programme or the areas being measured (note that in a large measurement programme there may be several review teams, each looking at different sets of information). The team also needs to appoint a leader, or chair, who will insist that the principles on which the group is intended to operate are rigorously applied.

It is possible to utilize such a team on the basis that they meet as and when necessary, but this is less effective than having fixed meetings at regular intervals, possibly tied to the reporting cycle. If the group decides occasionally to cancel a meeting, or has to positively think about whether or not to convene a meeting, important indications may well be missed or at least not picked up until long after the appropriate time for action.

Employing such a team, though, does mean that matters will move more slowly than if the task is allocated to an individual. Analysis will have to wait until the team can meet and may be slowed down by differing opinions or agendas amongst team members.

REVIEW CHAMPION

The alternative is to appoint a single person, a 'champion', for the review process. (Note that the term 'champion' is also sometimes applied to the senior manager who supports the programme at the highest level, ensuring that resources are made available as needed.) All reports are sent to this single person who decides what the results mean, what should be done about them, and then passes on the issues arising to the appropriate person for action.

This technique is efficient in time and resources. An individual can come to conclusions more quickly than a team, and problems associated with pulling the group together for meetings or having to deal with differing underlying agendas and motives are avoided. Moreover, reviews can be conducted as and when required without having to fit in with the appointed meeting schedule.

It can also be highly time-efficient in terms of concentrating attention where it is most needed; the single, expert reviewer will quickly become proficient at examining the data and identifying areas that do or do not need attention. This avoids time wasted in debating sets of results that are meaningless but still engender debate simply because a meeting has been called for that very purpose. As long as the person has enough respect and authority in the organization to make things happen when and if necessary, then appointing a single, central champion can offer a fast and incisive system.

There are, however, some disadvantages to this approach. An individual can lose the broader picture and can quickly become attached to one or two personal ideas of what represents an issue to be tackled and what does not. Also, their ability to draw on a wide perspective and understanding is more limited than that of a team, risking the possibility of missing something important. Additionally, decisions or conclusions made by one person can be resented by those not involved in the decision process, even if the conclusion is one that they might have reached themselves.

A PRACTICAL APPROACH

A sensible way of dealing with this dilemma is to amalgamate the two approaches mentioned above. An individual is appointed to make an initial scan of the measurements, who then calls a predefined team together to address the main areas of interest already identified. This permits speedy initial response to any change or perturbation yet also retains the broad viewpoint offered by the analysis team.

This approach can be improved even further by appointing a range of individuals to act as the initial trigger or filter, each one covering a small range of measurement reports so that they are not overburdened with work and the programme is not dominated by the perspective of any one individual.

The people who perform the initial review and the team members should, wherever possible, be chosen from a pool of volunteers. Many staff will be unfamiliar with measurement, and many managers may be particularly uncomfortable with the measurement of people. For these reasons, conscripts to the project may perform less well than desired, so only highly willing participants should be used. It is better to have an enthusiastic person who needs some guidance working in the scheme than to insist on using specific technical experts who have no interest in the project.

The way in which this approach works is laid out in Figure 9.1.

The mixture of individual speed and flexibility and the strength of group support provides for a good method of using people measurement results.

BASELINING

Baselining is one of the simplest and most obvious tools to help identify when there is something happening that needs action. This involves establishing the measurement system and simply letting it run for a while, without using the initial data as a basis for investigation and action. The set of data thus

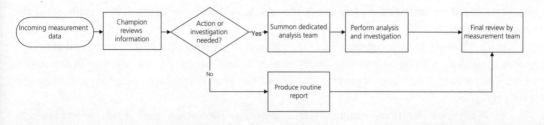

Figure 9.1   Measurement analysis by champion and team

collected is then used to provide an indication of what the people in the organization are doing so that subsequent measurements can be compared to that baseline.

This is an important concept since many of the measurements taken will not represent absolute values. While some elementary measurements (such as time lost through absenteeism) may be capable of being compared to statistics from another organization, many will simply be something that has been determined to be an indicator of feelings or behaviours and will only be meaningful when compared to itself. In such cases a baseline is vital for understanding whether any individual measurement is good or bad.

Let us, for example, consider a measurement that tries to determine the belief in business ethics existing in the workplace. Since the answer to this will depend on the way in which the measurement is taken and the scale of measurement that is used, we will only know how people think if we first take a 'reading', then take further readings later, either regularly or to mark key events. If the belief factor rises, we know that support for ethical practices is increasing; conversely, a downward movement would indicate that the belief is decreasing.

Although it is possible simply to use early sets of data to provide the baseline, some measurement programme teams conduct a specific exercise to gather baseline data before the 'real' measurement programme begins in earnest. This can waste time and effort in a system where people measurement is a proven and accepted practice, but could be valuable, for example, in cases where either the project team or the people being measured are uncertain about the whole exercise, because it is clear that no action will be taken on initial results and that subsequent data will only be considered in relation to early baselines.

> TIP
>
> If deciding to have an initial period just for baselining, watch out for cunning elements who wish to 'use' the system by creating artificially poor results for the baseline, so that subsequent performance indicators automatically show an improvement.

SURVEY AND INTERVIEW BASELINING

Where the measurement is being taken via survey (and, to some extent, by interview), finding a reference point for the intrinsic value of the measurements obtained becomes more complicated. On the one hand, baselining is more difficult to achieve because the task of conducting the survey is so large that one does not wish to conduct it twice in quick succession, yet, on the other hand, it is important because the exercise is so costly that the results must be immediately understandable, relevant and usable.

There are really only two choices here: either accept the relative nature of surveys and appreciate that full analysis may not be possible until the second one, or carry out a separate benchmarking exercise as part of the first survey programme. Both these alternatives have their own advantages and disadvantages.

Surveys are not absolute measurements in that, by their very nature, they are intended to measure opinions and feelings. Therefore if we simply take the results of the very first survey that we conduct at face value, the measurements on their own will tell us very little. If, for example, the average level of role and responsibility clarity turns out to be 6.2, we have no idea whether this is good or bad, since we do not know the internal benchmark that respondents have used to score their answers. We can, however, compare this value to those of other questions. Thus, if we find that role clarity is 6.2 but opportunity for personal training and development is 8.9, then it is quite clear that our employees are less happy about the definition of responsibilities than they are about the opportunities presented for training. In this way, the first choice can be quite valid, since we can see how one question's response compares to that from another question, without having to understand the absolute level. Validity is enhanced when we also use analysis of the gap between desire and reality, as we can then more easily see where employees believe that there is a shortfall. This is possible because we are using the employees themselves to provide the measuring stick, working on the assumption that an employee will regulate themselves in order to ensure that relative responses are correctly scaled (a reasonable assumption, since employees are very unlikely to change their yardstick at each question).

If we try to follow the second option, that of conducting a separate benchmarking survey, this has a number of disadvantages, as spelt out in Table 9.1.

Table 9.1   Disadvantages of separate baselining surveys

Disadvantages

- The start of the actual survey is delayed.
- The baseline survey occupies valuable management time.
- It makes the people surveyed less enthusiastic for the second, 'real' survey.
- Baselining is not a completely accurate form of calibration.
- The data so painfully gathered for the baselining survey cannot be used to initiate action.
- The baseline is meaningless if circumstances change between the baseline survey and the 'real' one.

The only possible advantage it could have is to provide a scale against which subsequent results can be measured. Even this, though, does not exist. If the baselining exercise is conducted for a limited set of questions, it still leaves the question unresolved for those questions left unmeasured. If it is carried out for a limited audience, then the value of self-regulating scales is lost since it is possible for the subpopulation chosen to have a different scale than the full population (for example, we may have unwittingly chosen for the limited sample all those employees who exhibit particularly pessimistic attitudes and whose scores are all, therefore, unrealistically low). For the pure questionnaire survey, therefore, the baselining exercise has no benefits and many drawbacks and should thus be avoided.

Trying to conduct a baselining exercise as part of an interview programme has all of the disadvantages mentioned in Table 9.1. Indeed, some of the drawbacks may be enhanced, especially if external consultants are used to help conduct the interviews, in which case the timescales and costs will certainly increase. In contrast to surveys, however, there is some possibility of creating valid data from a limited set of people. Using interviews as measurements relies more on the interviewer establishing the scale than on the person being measured. Thus it is possible to create a passable, if not 100 per cent accurate, baseline by interviewing a more limited sample than the actual chosen set. However, the disruption that these exercises cause and the effort involved mean that trying to conduct a separate measurement exercise purely for the purpose of baselining is probably not really worth the effort.

CONCLUSIONS ON THE ADVISABILITY OF BASELINING

Conducting a separate exercise to create a baseline against which subsequent measures can be evaluated is only appropriate for continuous monitoring; it does not sit well with the other measurement techniques. Yet, with continuous monitoring, creating an even baseline as a separate exercise is not really worthwhile. While it is vital to have a foundation against which measurements can be compared, the best approach, as I stated right at the beginning of this section, is to simply let the measurements run for a while before leaping on them to make decisions. As a general rule, two or three sets of data are needed before anyone can begin to consider whether the measurements indicate anything actionable.

Bear in mind that the baseline will have to be regularly reviewed. If improvements are made, the working environment changes, there have been staff movements or other factors arise that indicate that things may not have remained static, we will need to reconsider what the current baseline should be. This will also apply to measurements that *do* have some fixed standard. For instance, if we are measuring absenteeism, we should not only compare the results against what we have experienced in the past but also against industry norms; if we are roughly level with what everyone else experiences, we can be satisfied with small improvements but if we are lagging behind something more substantial may be called for. This will involve regularly looking at what is happening in the industry to revisit, and if necessary change, our idea of what the baseline is.

COMPARATIVE AND ABSOLUTE TARGETS

THE NEED TO SET TARGETS

A usual approach with any measurement is to set targets. These help us to see whether the behaviours and performance that we are monitoring are somewhere near what we hope for, assist with determining trends, provide goals for those taking action and help with identifying those areas that most urgently need the attention of the improvement teams.

ABSOLUTE TARGETS

The most desirable set of targets is an absolute set that can be established in terms of real expectations. For example, if I stay with the absenteeism example used earlier under the discussion of baselines, we could find out what the local industry average was for absenteeism, in terms of percentage or working days lost per year, and then set that as our initial target. Alternatively, we might decide that we would like at least ten people to attend each of our lunchtime seminars to make them viable and define our target at that level. If our measurement can be considered to be absolute, the target should also be absolute, so that the target is set at a level representing the state at which we hope our organization will perform.

This can be the start of a difficult thinking process. The first problem is understanding where the level sits in relation to absolute performance levels. This in turn will involve considering what other organizations are doing and how the world at large performs. This is something that many organizations do not even attempt to consider and that some are even frightened of thinking about. Where people are concerned, there are, broadly speaking, two types of organization: those that just attempt to get by and concentrate on getting today's tasks done and those that try hard to create the best working environment to enable them to produce the best results. Even for the second type of organization, it is difficult to establish what everybody else is doing; for the first type, it is even harder to find the time to appreciate at what level they should set their targets. Nevertheless, this difficult topic must undoubtedly be tackled. If we have no understanding of our hoped for performance level, the measurements that we take have far less value. Thus it is worth making the effort to identify the level at which an organization such as ours is expected to perform and set our targets accordingly.

Just a word of caution, though. Beware of assuming that the best target is one that reflects the very best industry practice. Although this might be a valid target for our business in some cases, in others it may not be appropriate. If we know that we are weak in a specific area (which may be one of the reasons why we are measuring it) then it makes no sense to set a target that is simply unachievable. Granted, this may be suitable as a long term stretch-goal, but our measurement target needs to be something more immediate.

RELATIVE TARGETS

In a way, relative targets are easier to set. Where our measurements do not relate to any externally meaningful factors, then our targets simply cover how we wish to be relative to where we are now, or where we have been. At the very simplest level, we just look at the measurement values in areas (perhaps after having baselined them) and decide to set a target at a suitable level. If we are moderately happy with what we are measuring, we may set our target to indicate a minimum level at, or just below, what we are currently experiencing.

Conversely, if it is an area that we feel needs to be improved (there may be reasons for improvement other than measurement, such as customer complaints or cost reduction drives), we set our target to show a suitable proportionate improvement. A word of caution here, though. Any target should be at least of the same order of magnitude as our current measurements. If the level is set too distant from our current position, any graphical representation of the result will be difficult to read and will be disheartening for those involved; equally, if the target seems impossibly far away, we may just give up any hope of reaching it (this applies also to absolute measurements). If we want to make an enormous improvement, the best approach may be to set interim targets and move forward in incremental steps – after all, anyone can eat an elephant but it needs to be done one bite at a time.

SINGLE AND DUAL TARGETS

For each measurement, it must be determined whether single or dual targets are required. A dual target is where both maximum and minimum boundaries are set such that it is intended that the measurement should fall between the two. This is routinely used in manufacturing where an item must be between a maximum and minimum size in order to fit well with another item; another example might be in food packaging, where the minimum quantity must be at least the weight stated on the customer's packaging but should be below another weight to avoid overcompression of the product and to ensure that costs are minimized. A single target is where we are only interested in one end of the spectrum, such as answering the telephone within a maximum of three rings but within no minimum time, or setting a minimum sales target although selling too much is definitely not a problem.

When considering people measurement there are fewer examples of dual targets. We would, for instance, only set a desired minimum for a loyalty index since we cannot conceive of an employee being too loyal and would set a top limit for our absenteeism target since there is no lower limit below which we would be unhappy to fall. There will be some dual targets, however. Consider starting time: we may wish for employees not to arrive much later than the official start time but would not want them to arrive too early either since it could cause problems with security and access if they arrive very early or could result in large numbers going home before we wish them to as they have already fulfilled obligations in terms of hours worked.

For each measurement that we introduce, then, we will need to consider whether a single or dual target is appropriate and set them accordingly. A final point of warning: do not assume that dual targets should lie equidistantly from the nominal value. With respect to the arrival time example just discussed, we may wish to set our target for lateness at no more than 15 minutes behind the official start time, but our margin for early arrival might be much broader, allowing up to an hour before we consider that people are arriving too early. Each target, whether it is one of a pair for the same measurement or a target on its own, should be considered on its own merits before the value is set.

THE TARGETLESS APPROACH

One other possibility for a measurement system is to use the results and analyses without having targets against which to compare them. This can be a valid approach if, for example, the measurements are based on arbitrary indices that would produce completely relative targets with no obvious direct meaning, or where circumstances change too quickly for sensible targets to be set based on prior measurements or baselines.

The conclusions that can be drawn from a measurement that is not being compared to a target are more limited than those where targets are being used. They can, however, still be effectively used to determine:

- sudden 'blips' or step changes
- upward or downward trends
- seasonal or other attributable variations
- relative levels between one group of people and another.

These can be extremely useful to see how much effect an initiative is having. If, for example, we have a general feeling that we need to improve in a certain area but the only way in which we can enumerate the people-based activity is to create an arbitrary index, comparing the measurement to a target may not tell us much; however, we can see if our efforts are succeeding by monitoring whether the index shows an improvement over time.

In summary, where target setting seems too difficult, it is possible to collect and use measurement data without one. My own preference, though, is to set targets wherever and whenever possible since it provides an extra dimension of information that cannot be achieved from just looking at the measurement alone – for example, if our index is showing a gradual improvement but we are still a very long way from where we want to be, we may need to adjust our programme to create faster improvement, but without a target we may not realize this.

IDENTIFYING AREAS FOR ACTION

UNDERSTANDING WHERE TO ACT

As I have constantly emphasized, the only real purpose for measuring people is to enable us to take some action when and where needed. This means that our measurement programme must enable us to easily identify the 'where and the when'. This is achieved in different ways depending on the type of measurement being evaluated and the maturity of the programme.

IMMATURE PROGRAMMES

In a highly immature measurement regime – that is, one that has only just begun and has, as yet, produced few results – the choice of where to take action is easy. The first actions should be those aimed at improving areas about which people feel most strongly. This is for two reasons:

● Those being measured will lose faith in the process if it does not address what they perceive as the most important issues.
● The areas about which people feel most strongly will also be those that have the most immediate impact on morale and loyalty.

Be warned that these areas are not necessarily those that seem the most important from the perspective of corporate management. For example, the head of human resources may see the issues of staff turnover and absenteeism as being of the greatest immediate concern, yet the employees themselves may see inadequate toilet facilities or lack of crèche facilities as being those elements that provide them with the most stress.

Nevertheless, the issues tackled first and with the greatest alacrity must be those that measurements revealed to be of the greatest concern to employees, even if they are not seen as being the top management priority. Only after the top three employee priorities have been addressed can the management agenda begin to be tackled.

These areas will be most obvious where the survey or interview measurement methods have been chosen. Certainly a gap analysis will reveal where the workforce imagines the largest difference between desired and actual states to exist. Simply by noting where these are, the areas needing immediate action can be pinpointed. Note that some intelligence needs to be applied to this review; look carefully at the raw data as well as the resultant gap. One measurement may, on a scale of 1 to 10, show a desired state of 4 and perceived state of 1, giving a gap of 3, where another may show a desired level of 9 with a perceived state of 6, also giving a gap of 3. They are not, however, the same. The first is a situation where the company is not performing that well but is an area about which people do not really care that much, whereas the second represents a situation about which people care a lot but in which the company is only showing mediocre performance. Consequently, the second case requires far greater attention than the first.

Where continuous measurement is being applied, identifying the areas of greatest employee concern is less straightforward because this technique is more about measuring behaviours than feelings. Thus, although we may well see the results of what people believe is important in their own actions, it is more difficult to see what they feel strongly about in the wider organizational environment. Even here, though, it is important to select initial action areas that address factors considered by the workforce to be most crucial. The analysis team need to bear this in mind and look for those indicators that relate some dissatisfaction or discomfort with the status quo, rather than those that might be perceived as penalizing or admonishing the workforce.

All of this is not to say that a company should ignore key issues arising in the early days that will have a direct impact on effectiveness or efficiency. For example, any of the measurement techniques might reveal that confidentiality of information is not taken seriously by many people, yet will have a great impact on the company's future success. Such an issue must, of course, be addressed. What is important, however, is to appreciate that those issues which make the employees feel positive about the initiative must figure strongly in the early action phases. It is not uncommon to find out, for example, that employees feel that their roles are not clearly enough defined, and this can lead to overlaps (inefficiency) and gaps (ineffectiveness). Remedying this by definition, communication and training will both reduce stress for employees and help eliminate the attendant inefficiency and ineffectiveness. It should also be borne in mind that most employees are not simply selfish, lazy money-grabbers; many of the issues that they are unhappy about will represent factors which they feel are obstructing them in doing a good job, which is what most people want to feel able to do. ·

MATURE PROGRAMMES

Surveys and interviews

In a mature survey or interview measurement regime, where a number of data sets have been collected, the focus can be directed more on those elements that lead to business improvement rather than on simply enhancing employee morale. This is not to say that those issues perceived as important by the employees can be ignored – once people have been 'won over', the programme must keep delivering employee satisfaction in order to maintain their trust. The difference is that a mature programme can concentrate on business performance issues as the first priority, while keeping in mind that employee morale will always need to be a factor in corporate decisions.

Identifying those areas where action needs to be taken in surveys is relatively easy; the target list simply contains those areas with the largest gaps, referenced against the list of those areas with the lowest satisfaction scores. When the largest gaps/poorest scores have been dealt with, those with the next most serious results are considered, and so on, until we reach areas where the results of the survey indicate that action is not necessary (or where the indicated need for action is too low to make it worthwhile).

Continuous measurement

Measurements in a continuous monitoring programme provide the most scope for detailed analysis of action need but also present us with the greatest complexity of choice and decision-making. Their greatest benefit is that they are, by definition, continuous and therefore offer a regular set of data telling us, for example, how one particular set of behaviours is developing. By contrast, the one-shot nature of interviews and surveys can mean that, despite our best efforts, the results from one cycle cannot be directly compared with those of the previous cycle.

We can make use of this prolific stream of data to present our information graphically. There is no need to do anything incredibly sophisticated here; simple line graphs or barcharts showing each measurement will suffice. For those who are not familiar with drawing such graphs (that is, they have forgotten, through lack of use, those skills painfully learnt in the mathematics classrooms of their youth), they can very easily be generated using any modern spreadsheet program by simply placing the sequential data values in a row, selecting the row and selecting the 'chart' feature in the program. I prefer the line chart for this type of measurement because it provides the clearest indication of changes and trends, but often it is a matter of taste. However, beware of trying to be too clever here.

There are many techniques used for creating and displaying graphs such as moving average approaches and cumulative-sum methods. There is nothing wrong with using these if you fully understand them and have a good reason for using them in a particular situation. Bear in mind, however, that many of these methods are designed to draw the best out of exact measurements which may be inappropriate when we are dealing with organisms rather than precise data. The same applies to the various statistical techniques that might be espoused; although they are very useful when used correctly, remember that they are only as good as the raw data. In many cases, some of these techniques can be used to assist in the overall understanding of the data (indeed, I touch upon some of them in this book) but they should be simply for the internal use of the analysis team and not intended for routine, general publication. Although there are discussions in this book about how to make your data consistent and reliable, remember that the exercise involves people measuring people and is not a precise art.

> **TIP**
> If you do want to use some basic statistical techniques but want to keep it simple, it is possible, again, to use a spreadsheet to do the hard work without you having to become an expert number-cruncher. Once this is done, a simple Internet search will reveal many websites (most of them from university and other academic sources) explaining, in simple terms, how to perform simple statistical tests, such as checking whether recent samples look different to the main population.

Once you have a graph of ongoing measurements it is not too difficult to identify where something is happening that needs attention. Examples of this could be:

- consistent failure to achieve target (see Figure 9.2)

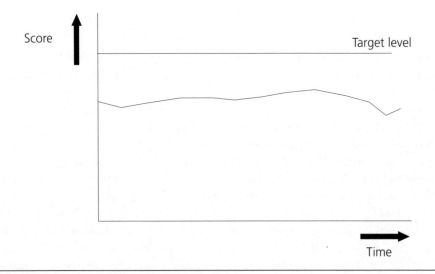

Figure 9.2　Consistent failure to achieve target

- highly variable results (see Figure 9.3)
- worsening trends – for example, where we are achieving our target but the safety margin is decreasing with time (see Figure 9.4)
- 'spikes' or 'blips' (see Figure 9.5).

Where we are consistently failing to meet a target, we must review first whether both our data and target are correct (often a large mismatch between the two indicates a measurement, rather than actual, problem). If the picture is accurate, something obviously needs to be done to bring reality closer to our desired position.

If our results are highly variable, it is vital to change the way in which things are managed (or, perhaps, measured) in order to create a more stable environment. If our people are placid one day and irritable the next, the whole working environment will deteriorate. This also makes the actual level of our measurement difficult to determine and can cause us to miss overall changes in level that are hidden in 'the noise'. Any attempt at overall process improvement will also be difficult to monitor since we will not be able to immediately tell whether a movement is due to our efforts or to normal variation. Thus a widely varying set of results should encourage us to work towards ways of making the process more stable and reliable.

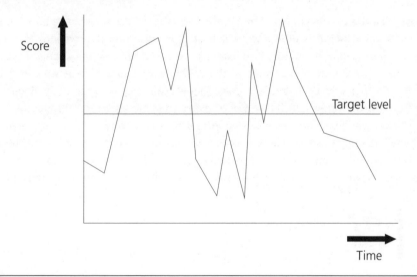

Figure 9.3   Highly variable results

If our measured level is deteriorating then we obviously need to do something about it. An increase in the number of visits to the personnel officer to 'have a moan' about colleagues or bosses would be a cause for concern, even if the overall level is still not that high, since it indicates that something is getting worse or is causing a problem and needs to be resolved. Only by investigating the reason for the deterioration and doing something about will we avoid bigger problems in the future.

'Blips' are often seen as unimportant. Indeed, politicians and business leaders often try to explain away a problem by describing it as 'just a blip'. By this, they mean that it is a situation of limited duration that does not reflect the overall trend. Although, to some extent, this is reasonable, it does not mean that blips can be ignored. A single or short-lived deviation from a steady situation or trend must have been caused by something – and that something might either be extremely significant and

Figure 9.4   Worsening trends

contribute to overall levels or drifts or could be a real one-off that will never occur again. The problem is that we do not know which it is unless we look at it. It is important that we look at each spike, understand why it occurred and what its implications are. If we can link the change in level to an extreme or completely rare occurrence, such as the death of the head of state, we can reasonably assume that it will have an effect on people but also that we can effectively ignore it, since it will not happen that often. On the other hand, if the blip relates to something more mundane, such as a heatwave, then we can anticipate that we will have several hot spells every year and cannot just accept that our people will display lower levels of cooperation, for instance, every time that the weather becomes a bit warmer. To re-emphasize, we must investigate and understand the root cause of every blip or spike and assess whether it is truly a one-off or is something that may be repeated and needs to be dealt with.

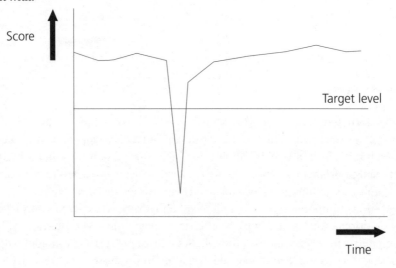

Figure 9.5   Measurement 'blips'

ACTION PLANNING

IDENTIFYING OPTIONS

Once we have identified that there is a situation that requires action, we have to consider exactly what action we need to take. When we are dealing with people this is not always obvious; if we were dealing with the products of a machine shop that we had discovered were too large, we would obviously need to start making them a little smaller, perhaps by adjusting the settings on our machine. If we find something like a belief problem, however, our options may not be quite so immediately clear. Let us consider that our measurements indicate that the workforce do not trust regular management announcements and treat them with a large degree of cynicism. Dealing with this is not as easy as adjusting the machine settings. It requires careful thought and planning.

The usual suspects in terms of problem-solving should be dragged in under such circumstances. Techniques such as brainstorming, where a group uses free-thinking and idea association to identify possible ways of dealing with the situation or problem, come into their own here. There are other ways of doing the same, often based on the basic principles of brainstorming and all of which are commonly understood in industry, so I do not propose to list or describe them at length here. If your own organization already has a preferred problem-solving tool, or you are particularly fond of one of these methods, then I suggest you use that one.

The point here is, though, that a strong list of potential ways of addressing a measurement action indicator needs to be generated in order to ensure that an effective solution to the problem is found. Certainly it is worth taking time over this; do not rush into immediate actions that have not been thought through. I was recently involved with a company in which the sales director felt that the staff did not express much loyalty and was particularly concerned that this feeling might be apparent to visiting potential customers. Prior to an important visit, he gathered as many of the staff together as he could and told them that they had all better show more loyalty or woe betide them. Clearly, such knee-jerk reactions will have little effect on the problem and can even make things worse.

It is also important not to try to decide on a solution alone. Developing a plan that will change the behaviours and beliefs of one or more people is not a trivial matter and will probably need the support and input of the entire management or champion team, not just an admonishment by the sales director or any other individual, no matter how laudable or worthy their intentions. This is why the old favourite, brainstorming, is so good for the task. By its very nature it requires the involvement of several people and it also generates a wide range of options. The very reason for its popularity is that it has been proved to be an effective and reliable tool.

My favoured approach, then, would be for a champion to identify areas that are likely to need attention and pass these on to a suitably authoritative team which confirms the need for action. The team would then conduct a brainstorming exercise to generate a large, random set of ideas from which they develop a shortlist of possible avenues to explore.

PICKING THE BEST OPTION

The method used to choose the best option from the final shortlist should be more sophisticated than some form of simple ranking or voting exercise. Such techniques are best used in situations where the consequences are reasonably predictable and, frankly, a less than best choice can be suffered – determining which brand of telephone system to buy, for example. Where people are involved, though, we are playing with deep forces such as emotion and pride; insensitivity or blunder when addressing them can lead to longlasting damage that may never quite be repaired. Selecting the best of the possible options, just as with choosing the options themselves, needs careful thought and consideration of what the action will mean, what it will achieve and what the possible consequences will be, both directly and via side-effects.

This will call for some form of risk and benefit analysis. For each option, the team making the final decision will need to understand what the action involves, how long it will take, what it is intended to achieve, how well it addresses the initial problem or measurement deviation, the probability of success, and what could go wrong and how likely that is. This precludes a simple decision immediately following the brainstorming session; the best option can only be achieved by careful analysis and consideration, balancing likely success with risks and other implications.

The best option may not necessarily be the easiest or most obvious. Our natural tendency might be to loudly admonish somebody (rather like a parent with anger at a child) when we detect anything undesirable, but this is hardly likely to achieve anything more than an extremely temporary change in behaviour. The best option from the list is likely to be one that offers little immediate righteous gratification but takes a longer-term view. This, in turn, usually means tackling the underlying problem rather than the signs and symptoms. Our measurements will have revealed the signs and symptoms of a problem; our task is to dig deeper and address the root cause of these. If the employees in an organization have demonstrated, in some part of our measurement programme, that they do not trust statements by senior managers, then simply encouraging or instructing them to have greater trust will not do the trick. The solution is to make the managers demonstrably more trustworthy and the trust, properly nurtured, will naturally follow. Similarly my sales director introduced under 'Identifying Options' would have done better to work with the whole team to create a culture of improved mutual loyalty, rather than simply tell people that they needed to be more loyal.

COST–BENEFIT CONSIDERATION

I need to address the topic of cost–benefit comparison here, since it is commonly used by organizations embarking on new projects of any sort – including, perhaps, actions resulting from measurement indicators. Again, it is important to remember that standard accountancy practices cannot be applied to issues concerning people. If we are embarking on a programme aimed at encouraging employees to be more positive about the company's (and hence their) future prospects, it is, of course, possible to calculate how much will be spent in time, materials and resources on conducting that programme. However, it is impossible to directly calculate the likely financial benefit from having a more positive working environment. There will undoubtedly be some benefits, but these are enablers to better performance in other areas, rather than providers of direct benefits in themselves.

If, however, we try to step aside from the purely financial approach, we can try to conduct a review that is meaningful. For anything that we are aiming to do – correcting a problem, improving a situation, enhancing our capabilities and so on – there will be a reason for doing it. So, before we decide to embark upon a project it is worth understanding what the desired outcome will be and what, in qualitative terms, it will mean to us, including any likely positive side-effects. Then we can go on to consider the costs, what time and effort it will take, whether the project will have deleterious effects in other areas and what the consequences might be if things go wrong (in fact, such an exercise is strongly linked to the risk assessment mentioned below). Finally, we can consider whether the likely benefits are worth the 'costs'. This technique can also be useful for deciding between a number of options for tackling the result of measurements.

Of course, this form of analysis can never be as definite as a wholly financial cost–benefit exercise. When just looking at money we can, once the accounting conventions have been agreed crunch the numbers and come up with two figures. If the benefit figure is larger than the cost figure (or represents an adequate payback time and so on) then the project is favoured; if not, then it will have a hard time gaining approval – although I accept that there can be disagreements here that make such an analysis less absolute than might at first be thought. With a people-based analysis there may not be any numbers, just words. Under such circumstances the analysis is an aid to decision-making rather than providing a hard and fast 'yes' or 'no', but since this is generally true of all people measurements I am sure that readers are becoming used to this idea by now.

RISK ANALYSIS

For any course of action that is to be embarked upon, it is a good idea to carry out a simple risk analysis before proceeding. As mentioned earlier, initiating actions with little forethought can do irreparable damage to relationships with employees, so it is worth considering first what their effects might be.

The basic approach is not dissimilar to that carried out for health and safety risk assessments, or even an engineering 'failure modes and effects analysis' (FMEA). The difference is that we are aiming to predict behaviours and personal impacts rather than physical events, so a little more creativity is required.

For each possible course of action on our shortlist, we should ask ourselves:

- Who will be disadvantaged by this?
- Will it affect anybody's standard of living?
- Will it mean more work (both long- and short-term) for anybody?
- Will there be any perceived loss of status?
- Are we dealing with previously recognized taboos?
- What other reasons might there be for somebody disliking this course of action?

For each potential problem identified through these questions, we must then ask:

- What form(s) might people's reaction take?
- Which people might have that reaction?
- How quickly will it occur?
- How long will it last?
- How likely is the reaction?

Finally, we can look at each possible or likely reaction and consider what steps we can take to eliminate or reduce the likelihood of it occurring and/or reduce its negative impacts on the workforce as a whole. This will result in a picture of the risks and possible outcomes of each of our courses of action, helping us to make the best decision. Then, when a specific action has been chosen, the exercise can be rerun to help us plan to negate or reduce any negative effects that it may have.

> TIP
> Be careful about the 'How long will it last?' question. It is very tempting, when finding that there is a potential downside to our favourite action plan, to say 'Oh, they'll soon get over it'. Do not underestimate the longevity of bad feeling and resentment; sometimes it can lay festering only to rise from its dormancy months later.

PROJECT PLANNING

Planning is an essential prerequisite for success. Once we know what we are going to do and the contingencies and safeguards that we wish to use, we need to plan our project.

Preparing a project plan typically involves:

- appointing an overall project leader
- appointing a project coordinator (possibly the leader) to plan and monitor the various tasks
- listing the tasks, including any action needed to reduce risk
- estimating the duration of each task
- identifying the dependencies of tasks – for example, we cannot begin fitting out the new employee rest area until it has been built
- producing an overall schedule – for complex projects this might involve a barchart (sometimes known as a Gantt chart) but it could just be a list of tasks with their intended start dates and hoped-for completion dates
- allocating somebody to be directly responsible for each task.

It may also be necessary to identify what resources will be needed by the project. This will not only include the money that will be spent but also such things as the need for time with expensive equipment, meeting rooms, 'loan' of certain people, interruption of work flows and so on.

Once the whole plan is in place, the project leader works with the project coordinator (if not the same person) to remind people to start tasks on time, to help fight for resources and commitment in the organization, to chase up deadlines and to deal with questions, barriers and problems that can arise. This can be very time-consuming and needs to be allowed for. No project of any complexity ever runs completely smoothly; we cannot just start things off and assume everything will turn out all right, and neither can we just allow individuals to go ahead with their tasks without overall support, management and coordination.

MONITORING AND FOLLOW-UP

I have already mentioned that the undertaking of any action resulting from a measurement indicator needs to be monitored as part of project management to ensure that it is implemented in accordance with an agreed plan. What about the results of the action, though?

Once we have carried out our intended action to tackle a people issue, the bad news is that we cannot sit back and congratulate ourselves. If life were simple, we could perform an act that is intended to achieve a result and be certain that the result would be achieved. Sadly, life is not like that. I am sure our ancestors would have liked to have been able to throw a spear at a wild boar and then turn away, knowing that the job was done; in practice they had to check for success or be killed by an enraged beast. Similarly, we will need to see what effect our undertaking has really had. We must monitor the behaviours, attitudes and beliefs of our people to see whether they have been affected by our programme and, if so, whether the effect is in the right direction!

This is not just a tidying-up exercise and can have a number of benefits:

- It allows us to feel deserved pride if things have turned out well.
- It allows us to learn what works and what does not for future projects.
- It permits adjustment and addition to correct any problems or deviations that are spotted.

This last point is perhaps the most important. Since we know that thrown spears do not always land exactly in the spot that we intended, no matter how well we plan and consider the throw, there may well be facets of the response to our actions that are not as we would have liked. Monitoring and observing the results of the project give us the information that we need to take some extra action, or change an element or two, in order to bring events back on track.

In a regime of continuous measurement such monitoring is easy; indeed, it is almost inherent in the system. After an initiative, we just carry on measuring the parameter that caused us to take some action in the first place and the output will show us whether our action has had any effect and what that effect is. All that is needed in this case is some way of marking on our measurement charts or tables the point at which the initiative took place and it is then relatively simple (after allowing some time for the effects to 'kick in') to continue to monitor and know when follow-up action should take place. If we are using surveys or interviews for our measurements, however, we have to do something positive to discover the effects of what we have done, and this will necessarily involve conducting another survey or interview. This does not need to be a full repeat programme, but can be conducted on a smaller sample, with a reduced set of topics or questions, designed specifically to identify the effects of the actions that have been taken. As long as it is done as impartially and professionally as the original interviews, and those surveyed or interviewed are fully informed as to what it is all about, the indications of the outcome can be obtained without excessive effort.

> TIP
>
> Be extra rigorous about the fair design of topics and questions for these monitoring surveys and interviews. It is temptingly easy to set something up that is intended to confirm what a wonderful job has been done, rather than gather valid, objective evidence.

SUMMARY

- The ultimate aim of a measurement programme is action.
- Analysis of measurement results is needed in order to determine what action to take.
- Analysis can be carried out by a team or by an individual, although a practical approach is often for an individual to conduct a first pass, then submit items needing attention to a wider group.
- Baselining to provide a standard against which to judge comparative measurements can be a useful tool but is only appropriate for some types of measurement and, even then, has limited appeal as a completely separate exercise.
- Setting targets for measurements is a good way of knowing how well something is performing and providing a first step towards identifying areas for action.
- The type and level of a target needs to be set appropriately for the measurement in hand.
- Priority should be given to early actions to tackle employee concerns rather than issues of business efficiency and control.
- Longer-term actions need to be identified by examining measurements for change, variation, deterioration or failure to meet targets.
- For each area needing action, care must be taken in understanding the options available, and a professional approach taken to choose the right course.

- When action has been identified, the risks and issues need to be considered and tackled.
- During implementation, strong project management must be applied to ensure that the programme is kept on track.
- Once an action is complete, some method of follow-up is needed to confirm its effectiveness.

CHAPTER TEN

Understanding and Using the Environment

INTRODUCTION

Using quantitative measurements to understand the attitudes, feelings and behaviours of people within the organization can lead to a far greater degree of understanding than simply using 'management feel' or other less formal approaches. Before the measurements can be properly used, however, it is essential to understand the background to them – the environment from which they arise. We have already discussed, in Chapter Nine, the fact that many measurements are relative and thus need to be compared to baselines, targets, earlier data or a combination of the three. It is also important to appreciate the circumstances under which the measurements arise; then we can consider our analysis and subsequent actions accordingly.

Having an appreciation of the external environment is, of course, essential for all types of measurement. If we are monitoring air temperature within our premises then we must, of course, take external, ambient temperature into consideration to fully appreciate how this affects our efforts to control internal temperature. In this case, the environment has a direct and important impact on the attribute that we are considering. A parallel approach needs to be applied to people measurements. While there exist many operational and technical measurements that are barely influenced by environmental factors (for example, the dimensions of a steel bar are very slightly affected by ambient temperature but the effect is negligible in most cases), people are always strongly affected by what is happening around them. Moreover, their reactions to the environment may not always be obvious. We know that a steel bar's diameter will increase with heat, or that office temperature will be influenced upwards by the ambient temperature. With people though (keeping with the heat theme), it is not always as easy to predict how they will react to a heatwave; will they become slower and more lethargic, or will the sunshine and warmth make them feel happier, healthier and thus more energetic?

There is also a greater number of factors that will change the way that people will react than for many other business measurements. Not only will events and situations in the workplace affect what people think and do, but they will also be affected by world, national and local disasters, the economy, the organization's prospects, changes in other areas, family matters, personal health – in fact, almost anything that might impinge upon a person's life will affect the way in which they approach their work.

Although we need to be aware of what is going on around us, it is well nigh impossible to take all of it into account when looking at organizational people measurements. We certainly, for example, cannot allow for the fact that one employee is distracted today because their son or daughter did not come home from an all-night party last night. The fact that we are not sure about how any people measurement will be affected by environmental factors also means that we cannot have a formula that allows us to adjust our measurements for these factors, as we may do to compensate for internal temperature readings for ambient temperature variation, for example. What is important, though, is to at least have an idea of what is affecting our measurements and that there are external factors that exist beyond our control. This can help us have the best possible chance of understanding what our measurements mean.

THE SHORT AND LONG TERM

Where people are concerned, the longevity of any feeling or behaviour is always uncertain since it can vary so much from one person to another. Some of us are very 'immediate' revealing our emotions straightaway but then forgetting about it almost immediately, while others let their emotions build, only showing a full reaction once things have reached a threshold level.

Nevertheless, there are general tendencies for the workforce as a whole that we can consider to be short- and long-term. Some sets of feelings and actions may well be deep-rooted so that it takes sustained initiatives to change them, whereas others may only be temporary and will inevitably 'blow over'. Being uncomfortable with a simple change, for example, is usually a short-term thing, especially if the change is technical and not personal. Introducing a new telephone system may make people uncomfortable for a while and may even initially reduce telephone answering and associated performance, but once they become used to it (provided that we have not chosen a dreadful system), satisfaction and performance should improve as the new features and benefits become accepted.

Often whether a measurement represents a short- or long-term situation will depend on the duration of the underlying cause of the measurement. If the salesforce are 'buzzing' because sales have been good, then they will just as easily crash in the face of poor figures the following month if the good figures were for a single month only. On the other hand, if we have had years of high sales it will take many months of poor sales before morale starts to drop since just a month or two will seem to be only a momentary falter in a great track record. Similarly, resentment at a draconian, unpopular decision will be quickly overcome if it comes against a background of excellent employee relations and is succeeded by further popular pronouncements, but if it is another in a long line of bad decisions it will take more than a magnanimous concession or two to restore everyone's faith.

What is important is to aim to understand whether the effect that our measurements are revealing is likely to be short- or long-term. Of course, it will take more measurements to actually verify it, but some form of analysis and prediction here can save later heartache. If what we are seeing is a long-term trend, we probably need to do something fundamental (and long-term) in order to correct it, whereas a short-term effect can, perhaps, be dealt with by something as simple as a little reassurance.

> TIP
> Be objective. Do not fall into the trap of thinking that 'they will get over it'. Instead, look carefully at the longevity of the underlying situation and be realistic about the duration of the currently observed effects.

TRACKING ENVIRONMENTAL FACTORS

A measurement team needs to learn what external factors will have an impact on the measurements being taken. Some of these will gradually become apparent as the programme develops; where issues arise and the root cause is investigated, that root cause will become known. There are others where business knowledge and common sense will allow us to anticipate what external factors will have an impact on the things that we are measuring. Through whatever means the factors become apparent, the team needs to list and define them.

Once we understand the environmental factors that affect our people, and more specifically the people elements that we are measuring, it is a logical step to want to monitor those factors. This enables us to better understand what is happening with our people and to correctly interpret measurements. For example, we may operate in a highly competitive industry where staff turnover is potentially high and there are other employers needing similar skill-sets located close by. In such circumstances, employee retention is important and it may well be one of our measurements. It would be a good idea here to measure the salaries, in comparison to our own, being paid by local competitors since this will have a significant impact on the retention rates amongst a highly mobile workforce.

We should probably do this wholeheartedly and set up a measurement programme for these factors. Merely being aware of them may not be good enough. For example, if our measurement results are lagging indicators (see the following section) with a long delay, it will be some time before poor results become apparent. At that point, it will not be simple to look back and remember what the external circumstances were at that time. If, on the other hand, we have a set of relevant measurement results, we can look back and see from our records exactly what the position was.

How extensively this is done is a matter of balance between value and resource. In order to track moving environmental factors, and do it well, we will have to pay significant attention to data gathering and analysis. Although the framework for such efforts will already have been established as part of the internal measurement programme, gathering the data externally is far trickier and more time-consuming than it is for internal measurements. It thus requires significant resources, which can only be justified where the value of the resultant information is seen to be vital to the success of the measurement project. This will usually mean that only the most influential factors affecting the most important measurements are likely to be able to be tracked.

Bear in mind that event-based factors will probably also need to be omitted from our external monitoring programme since they cannot really be tracked in the same way as routine factors. Whilst we can measure inflation, competitive salaries, qualification levels, house prices, political swings, temperature and humidity, public technophobia levels and so on, we cannot, in the same way, monitor crises, family deaths, terrorist actions and the like. These occur as and when they will, and are not part of a trend. If a loaded ferry carrying some of our employees sinks in mid-voyage, then this can hardly be added to the standard list of recent disastrous ferry sinkings, and neither can we consider the fact that our sales director has been caught trying to sell company secrets to a competitor as a routine statistic. These are one-offs and so will be obvious when they occur – what we need to do is ensure that we remain aware of them and remember that their occurrence will have a great impact on the feelings and connected behaviours of the workforce. We should not be surprised if general mistrust and suspicion are worse after the sales director has been caught than they were before.

LAGGING AND LEADING INDICATORS

LAGGING INDICATORS

One important aspect of measurements that we must consider is that it often takes time for events to filter through to results. Quite often, what we are looking at can have changed some considerable time before our results even show any signs of it. Similarly, actions that we take may seem to have no immediate impact on the data that we collect. This can be for a number of reasons:

1. What we are measuring actually relates to something that happened some time ago. An example of this might be survey results that relate to how satisfied people are with the performance appraisal

process. Since performance appraisal comprises discussion, review and a subsequent action plan, a survey conducted even straight after the latest round of interviews will still elicit reactions to the earlier, more complete round of appraisals.

2. The action only affects new things and leaves many existing situations unaffected. We might have decided to consult employees from now on before designing any work area, but this is not likely to have much effect on people whose work area is not currently being redesigned.

3. People take time to react to what has been done. Sometimes even though something has improved, it takes time for people to change. Let us imagine that the canteen is unpopular so that many office staff choose to go out to lunch. This may cause them to take longer lunch breaks than they should and could tempt some to overeat or indulge in alcohol, making them less productive in the afternoons. If we improve the canteen facilities and catering arrangements, the intention might be to draw people back to eating on the premises but they will not do so on the first day. Staying away from the canteen could well have become a habit that will take time (and a clear improvement in food and service quality) to alter.

Equally, we might find that our actions seem to have caused a deterioration, rather than an improvement. Certainly, traditional teaching on the effects of change suggests that overall morale will initially dive before gradually improving if the change is managed well. Although there are techniques for minimizing the negative impacts of change, there can be a dip in morale (or performance) following a change even if it has been specifically introduced to cure a problem. Let us say that we decide to buck current trends and move a set of people out of an open plan environment and into smaller offices, to minimize noise and distraction, reduce the tendency to chatter, to make local temperature control easier[1] and to allow for greater privacy of telephone conversations. When we first move people, even though it might be what they wanted, they are inevitably going to suffer from not knowing where their files now are, from disorientation and from the need to generally 'settle themselves in'. As a result, their early performance will inevitably deteriorate owing to the disruption and their morale may dip until they begin to feel more comfortable with the new situation.

4. The action is indirect and therefore will take longer to affect the measurements. Indirect actions do not necessarily tackle the issue itself but something that has an effect on the issue. The office moving and canteen facility examples above are a form of this. Another example could be where we tackle apparently excessive levels of stress by providing access to gymnasium facilities. Having access to such facilities does not, of itself, reduce stress but if those facilities are regularly used, then they could help employees to cope with it better. Tackling the problem directly would involve changing the working practices and/or workload in a way that actually removes some of the stress.

Where the action and objective are not directly linked, we must expect some delay between our action and anything happening to the measurements. When we provide the gymnasium facilities, the first measurable factor in which we will see a change should be the number of employees that regularly use such facilities. Our stress indicator, though, will take longer to show any resultant movement since it will require frequent use of the facilities for any effect to be revealed.

The important thing about lagging indicators is to know where they exist and to conduct our analysis and planning accordingly. This will usually mean that greater patience is needed where lagging indicator measurements are used.

1. I am amazed at how often I see adjacent people in an open-plan office where one has the fan on full blast because they are hot and the other has a heater at their feet because they are cold – maintaining appropriate overall conditions under such circumstances is impossible.

LEADING INDICATORS

The fundamental problem with lagging indicators is not that they take some time to show results but that they show historical information. Thus we are looking at what has happened in the past and is a 'done deal'. If we are measuring employee satisfaction, by the time that we see our measurements it is often too late to prevent dissatisfaction because it has already happened. This is the case even if the delay between the situation and the measurement is very small.

It would be so much better if we could have a measurement that showed us what was going to happen before it actually did, and this is where we can use some of the factors in our working environment to our advantage. No, we cannot rely on arcane practices to predict the future, but just as some lagging indicators show the indirect results of actions and circumstances, so there are measurements that can be selected to indicate what will subsequently happen in other areas. An obvious case is just to reverse the example mentioned above; if stress is a lagging indicator for gymnasium usage, then how much the gym faculties are used must be a leading indicator for stress.

If we can find the right set of indicators to measure we may be able to predict future problems and act to prevent them before they occur. Thus, for example, if we are concerned about employee stress, we may choose to measure hours worked per employee, workload (that is, volume per person) and health support factors (such as gym use, perhaps). If these start to change in the wrong direction, it is reasonable to suppose that stress will increase so we can do something about it. If, on the other hand, we try to measure stress by absenteeism, coffee consumption, employee complaints and so on, these are lagging indicators that will not reveal anything until people are already suffering from stress.

In general, leading indicators tend to be more indirect and less connected to the desired result than are lagging indicators. The gymnasium usage measurement, for example, could be a poor indicator because low usage might occur for a number of other factors such as fashion, competing physical activities or even just personal preference (Oscar Wilde is reputed to have said that 'a gentleman never exercises'). A good measurement programme will often have a balance of leading and lagging indicators to provide a sensible overall picture.

RATE OF CHANGE

SLOW CHANGES

How quickly things change is another consideration when looking at presented measurement data. An obvious occasion on which we might identify areas that need action is when a chart of measurements shows an incline; any incline at all may be an action indicator for dual-target measurements, but where that incline represents a deterioration in a single target measurement it is particularly worthy of attention. However, the incline may not be apparent if we have chosen our reporting or calculation method inadvisedly. Scale is the most obvious factor. Although we may have chosen a scale for our charts that allows for reasonable variation of our index, it is entirely possible that a change in one of our people factors will manifest itself only by very slow and gradual changes.

For example, we may monitor, through simple observation by managers and supervisors, the number of employees that work through their lunch breaks rather than spending their time in the canteen, driving into town and so on. This could be an indicator of enthusiasm and dedication to work, especially in an environment where it has been habitual for people to forego their breaks. If we are observing a workforce of 40 office staff (since they are more likely to have the opportunity and choice to spend their lunch break as they wish than are shopfloor staff) then a 1 per cent increase in lunchtime leisure taking would mean two extra lunch hours per week no longer devoted directly to the job. This would be easy to miss if we were looking at a chart that showed a scale large enough to cover all possible measurements, yet it may well be significant enough to mark a change that is, ultimately, undesirable. The answer here – where simply thinking about the measurement tells us that the level of change we may be looking for is small – is to choose a scale for the chart that allows us to see these small changes, rather than one that will serve us for all levels for years to come; we can always rescale next year if the fundamental level has changed significantly. Of course, we must be careful in such cases to ensure that we are not reacting to an understandable 'blip'. Using the same example, the run-up to the annual festive season may see people keen to visit the shops to buy extra food, decorations, presents and so on and they may be taking long lunch breaks simply to cope with shopping necessities rather than demonstrating any reduction in their dedication to the job. Only a sustained, or steadily increasing, change in the measurement offers certainty that a real change is taking place, even though the early amount of change might be very small.

Before moving on to the case of rapid changes, I ought to say something about the nature of the example chosen in this section to illustrate the point. While the taking of lunch breaks may well be used as an indicator of dedication, especially if used in conjunction with other measurements, I would not wish for any reader to conclude that I am in any way advocating that employers should discourage people from taking them. Rests and breaks are important for people's health and well-being, as well as for their work efficiency; no measurement and action programme should be aimed at reducing the rights or privileges of workers in this regard. Such things can, however, be monitored where a change in the level (rather than the absolute level) can be an indicator of change in attitude or approach by the people in the organization. In fact, any large measurement regime will inevitably throw up situations where the actual level of the factor being measured is less important than looking for the meaning behind any change in that level.

RAPID CHANGES

A trickier problem than slow change is rapid change. In these cases the factor that is being monitored could worsen substantially before the measurement process starts to reveal anything untoward. If the measurement used is continuous, this situation can be dealt with by identifying those measurements that are particularly sensitive and then ensuring that the measurements are taken, and the analysis, conducted, often and quickly enough to pick up the changes at an early stage. Company management and the measurement team will have to pay attention to these measurements, maintaining awareness of which they are, and perhaps reporting and considering these more often than other indicators.

Where surveys or interviews are used, the only way that a true, rigorous measurement regime can be maintained for a factor that changes rapidly is to conduct the surveys or interviews very frequently. This might be done on a limited scale, attempting just to consider the fast-changing aspects and leaving the more stable elements for less frequent measurements. In a small organization this cannot work at all since the population becomes 'surveyed out' and will stop giving valid answers to questions if asked too often. However, even where there is a large potential population where attempts can be made not to survey the same person too regularly, this still has drawbacks. For one thing, the survey and interview tend to rely on a broad series of questions designed to obtain an overall picture of how people feel about things (unlike continuous monitoring which looks more at behaviour). Although people may suddenly feel incensed or elated about something, when asked about it in a calm situation, they are more likely to provide responses that reflect their overall view in recent times, not necessarily their momentary reaction.

It is also worth realizing that many things that are prone to quick change are likely to change quickly in both directions. For example, a sales team that has worked hard on a prospect may feel incensed if the managing director decides not to pursue the opportunity any further for reasons of risk or resource availability. At that moment, their immediate feeling could be that they have little faith in, or support for, the judgement of their leader. If, however, the overall feeling is one of respect for the organization's leadership, the aggrieved response will be quickly forgotten and feelings should settle back down close to their normal level. If the decision has had a lasting effect, then this will show up in 'normal' measurements and can be dealt with accordingly.

In fact, this example illustrates the behaviour of most factors with rapid changes; the faster the change the more temporary it is likely to be. This means that measuring it in a way that attempts to trap the rapid deviations might be a distraction that produces misleading results. Although the foundation on which this book is based is that regular, objective measurement is a better tool than intuition, we must also realize that there are times when trying to make such measurements is neither sensible nor practical; this is why we go to such lengths to identify the right measurements and analyse them correctly. A category that involves factors that may be prone to sudden, large swings or blips, may well be inappropriate for formal measurement. If we feel that we need to watch out for such swings, it is better to do so via management vigilance rather than measurement. This is not to say that we should not measure these factors at all, but that the measurement should be used to identify slightly longer-term trends, or lasting effects of blips, rather than try to catch the sudden deviations themselves.

TRENDS AND BLIPS

UNDERSTANDING

I have said that trends and blips, especially sudden and recoverable blips, need to be treated quite differently. In order to be able to do this we must be clear at both planning and monitoring stages how these two phenomena behave and where the boundary between them lies.

BLIPS

'Blip' is a word much loved, at the time of writing, by politicians. They use it to mean that any deviation in national statistics, their popularity, the economy and so on is purely an arbitrary and temporary thing that need not concern the population at large because it does not reflect the 'real' situation. I have used the word in much the same sense; it represents a temporary deviation, usually attributable to a discoverable, single cause. On a chart of measurements it will appear as a spike, as we saw in Figure 9.5 (p. 118).

We must not, however, write them off as unimportant merely because they are temporary. Even in the case of politicians, the argument that, say, a one-month rise in the number of unemployed persons is meaningless because we are seeing an overall fall is not very comforting to someone who has lost their job that month. Dealing, as we for the most part are, on a smaller scale than most politicians, the event can be even more worthy of note. A blip may consist of an indicator in one month's measurement that reveals an increased inclination for employees to look for a new job outside the organization, perhaps as a result of some unwelcome event or decision made at the start of the month; although our measurement may show that the inclination to leave falls again the next month, this will be too late if a few of our best people have already left (it is always the best employees who find it easiest to secure another job). Indeed, the reduction in the measurement could be misleading; it might occur simply because those people who felt most like leaving have already gone!

Any temporary deviation will need some investigation. In Chapter Nine, we discussed how areas for investigation and action can be identified, and the interpretation of blips was covered there. However, we must also consider to what extent the blip is generated internally and how much it is due to some external, environmental factor. This will indicate what preventive action we should take; if the blip was generated internally, we might be able to look at how to ensure that the cause does not recur, but if it was externally generated, in most cases, all we can do is act to minimize the impact of such occurrences in the future. If, for example, our observed change in behaviour was due to an especially cold spell in the weather, or a rail strike, the management of the organization can do nothing to prevent these actually happening but can take measures to make future occurrences less painful. Of course, part of this analysis must be to look hard at the external environment and try to appreciate its patterns. If rail strikes are few and far between, we can assume that this is a true 'blip' and devote our attention to something more important but, if they are regular, making them easier to bear might make a big difference to employee loyalty.

Another aspect of the behaviour of blips is whether they are 'pure' blips, after which the measurement returns to its previous level, or whether the subsequent stable level differs from the original one. For example, blips in several measurements in response to the shock generated by the dismissal of the operations director may settle once people realize with hindsight that they should have seen it coming and that they knew about pending reorganizations anyway, but the fact the company is willing to dismiss somebody may have a smaller but lasting effect on employees' feelings of security and loyalty. Even if the blip is so rapid that we miss it, its long-term effects may still be detectable; these effects must be taken account of and their causes understood, just as for a blip itself.

TRENDS

In general, trends are easier to deal with than blips. Where a measurement indicates that a factor is getting steadily worse, confirmed over several measurements, clearly something has happened and we should find out what and try to do something about it. Even here, though, we must be aware of the environmental situation that might influence our measurement.

At its most extreme, an entire trend might be a result of some external factors. An example might be steadily worsening timekeeping which, after investigation, is found to be directly attributable to increased traffic caused by the burgeoning new housing estate springing up nearby (it is an interesting phenomenon that people seem to find it hard to adjust their leaving time to allow for troublesome car journeys to work – their leaving time is often closely bound up with getting the children to school, the leaving time of their partner, a long-established signal that it is time to leave, such as hearing the hourly pips on the radio and so on). This is nothing to do with the organization's own treatment of its people but is due largely to the fact that increased potential traffic not only makes journeys longer, but also less predictable. Although this may be an obvious example, it illustrates that some things that we measure may be influenced as much by what happens outside as by what we do inside the organization. Other cases may not be quite so obvious, but unless we make sure that we consider the environmental factors that may be involved, we may struggle to allocate a cause to something that simply is not there. In most such circumstances, we will find that environmental factors contribute to, but do not dominate, a trend. In such cases we need to be even more vigilant in ensuring that we take them into account, since they could be distorting or even masking the true picture – it is possible that a real trend is under way but our measurements do not show it because the effect is masked by the effects of one or more environmental factors.

Bear in mind that trends can also be cyclic (in effect, extended blips). We might observe that people display slightly more energy, for example, during the longer, warmer days of the summer (except when it is exceedingly hot, where the reverse might occur), or it might be noticed that employees with strong family commitments are more distracted towards the end of the summer term and during the long summer holidays. Again, we must be aware that it is external factors that are having an influence here and not jump to the conclusion that something has changed in the organization without first giving it careful thought. Such cyclic deviations will, typically, settle back down after a little time; no action is needed other than to keep an eye on things.

DEALING WITH INDIVIDUAL DEVIATIONS

TESTING FOR VARIATION

One difficulty encountered by anybody dealing with a set of measured data is how much to take account of each individual measurement. The first case is where we see a measurement result, arising from our next measurement cycle, that appears, at first sight, to be quite different to those previously encountered. It is relatively easy to see that this requires investigating if the measurement represents a 'blip' against an otherwise stable background, but if previous data has been somewhat variable it is hard to know whether this is just part of that background variability or whether it really represents a change.

Although I have tried to steer clear of mathematical techniques in this book, testing to see whether a set of data really does indicate a change can be done by using some fairly simple mathematics. In this respect, significance testing is a good tool to have up your sleeve (if that is not mixing my metaphors too much). It is certainly an aid to decision-making; since making decisions and taking action is what this technique is all about.

The significance testing tool that I will explain here is called the chi-square test (χ^2). It is used to determine the probability that a measurement or set of measurements is significantly different from what is expected. In order to do this, we use a simple formula and a look-up table. The formula uses the *variance* of both the new and the previous samples. Variance is a statistical expression of how much a set of measurements varies; an identical set of data would have no variance. It is not really necessary to know how variance is calculated; any modern spreadsheet program will calculate it for you from a set of data entered into cells. You will, of course, need to use the actual individual values from each person's survey, measurement or interview and not the calculated averages.

If V is the variance of all measurement data collected in the past and N is the variance of the data in the new measurement sample, χ^2 is calculated by dividing N by V, and multiplying the result by the number of measurements in the new sample (that is, if 30 people were interviewed to provide the new measurement, then the number in the sample is 30).

Then we need to look at the row in the look-up table (shown as Table 10.1) which represents the 'degree of freedom'. For our purposes, the degree of freedom is equal to the sample size, less one. So if we surveyed 30 people, the degree of freedom is 29. We can then look along this row and see how our calculated number compares to the values in the table. Let us say that our calculated χ^2 value turns out to be 39.55. As we look along the '29' row, the first number that is greater than our value is 42.5569. This appears in the probability column of 95 per cent. This means that there is a 95 per cent probability that our sample is an expected part of the overall set of data, thus indicating that we probably do not have any cause to think that we have seen a change.

This is a not too complex tool that can easily be set up in a spreadsheet and can be used over and over again without having to devote too much effort to understanding the mathematics. Be aware,

Table 10.1   Chi-squared distribution

Degrees of freedom	Probability								
	0.5%	1%	2.5%	5%	10%	90%	95%	97.5%	99%
1	.000039	.000157	.000962	.0039321	.0157908	2.70554	3.84146	5.02389	6.634
2	.0100251	.0202007	.0506356	.102587	.210720	4.60517	5.99147	7.37776	9.210
3	.0717212	.114832	.215795	.351846	.584375	6.25139	7.81473	9.34840	11.34
4	.206990	.297110	.484419	.710721	1.063623	7.77944	9.48773	11.1433	13.27
5	.411740	.554300	.831211	1.145476	1.61031	9.23635	11.0705	12.8325	15.08
6	.675727	.872085	1.237347	1.63539	2.20413	10.6446	12.5916	14.4494	16.81
7	.989265	1.239043	1.68987	2.16735	2.83311	12.0170	14.0671	16.0128	18.47
8	1.344419	1.646482	2.17973	2.73264	3.48954	13.3616	15.5073	17.5346	20.09
9	1.734926	2.087912	2.70039	3.32511	4.16816	14.6837	16.9190	19.0228	21.66
10	2.15585	2.55821	3.24697	3.94030	4.86518	15.9871	18.3070	20.4831	23.20
11	2.60321	3.05347	3.81575	4.57481	5.57779	17.2750	19.6751	21.9200	24.72
12	3.07382	3.57056	4.40379	5.22603	6.30380	18.5494	21.0261	23.3367	26.21
13	3.56503	4.10691	5.00874	5.89186	7.04150	19.8119	22.3621	24.7356	27.68
14	4.07468	4.66043	5.62872	6.57063	7.78953	21.0642	23.6848	26.1190	29.14
15	4.60094	5.22935	6.26214	7.26094	8.54675	22.3072	24.9958	27.4884	30.57
16	5.14224	5.81221	6.90766	7.96164	9.31223	23.5418	26.2962	28.9454	31.99
17	5.69724	6.40776	7.56418	8.67176	10.0852	24.7690	27.5871	30.1910	33.40
18	6.26481	7.01491	8.23075	9.39046	10.8649	25.9894	28.8693	31.5264	34.80
19	6.84398	7.63273	8.90655	10.1170	11.6509	27.2036	30.1435	32.8523	36.19
20	7.43386	8.26040	9.59083	10.8508	12.4426	28.4120	31.4104	34.1696	37.56
21	8.03366	8.89720	10.28293	11.5913	13.2396	29.6151	32.6705	35.4789	38.93
22	8.64272	9.54249	10.9823	12.3380	14.0415	30.8133	33.9244	36.7807	40.28
23	9.26042	10.19567	11.6885	13.0905	14.8479	32.0069	35.1725	38.0757	41.63
24	9.88623	10.8564	12.4011	13.8484	15.6587	33.1963	36.4151	39.3641	42.97
25	10.5197	11.5240	13.1197	14.6114	16.4734	34.3816	37.6525	40.6465	44.31
26	11.1603	12.1981	13.8439	15.3791	17.2919	35.5631	38.8852	41.9232	45.64
27	11.8076	12.8786	14.5733	16.1513	18.1138	36.7412	40.1133	43.1944	46.96
28	12.4613	13.5648	15.3079	16.9279	18.9392	37.9159	41.3372	44.4607	48.27
29	13.1211	14.2565	16.0471	17.7083	19.7677	39.0875	42.5569	45.7222	49.58
30	13.7867	14.9535	16.7908	18.4926	20.5992	40.2560	43.7729	46.9792	50.89
40	20.7065	22.1643	24.4331	26.5093	29.0505	51.8050	55.7585	59.3417	63.69
50	27.9907	29.7067	32.3574	34.7642	37.6886	63.1671	67.5048	71.4202	76.15
60	35.5346	37.4848	40.4817	43.1879	46.4589	74.3970	79.0819	83.2976	88.37
70	43.2752	45.4418	48.7576	51.7393	55.3290	85.5271	90.5312	95.0231	100.4
80	51.1720	53.5400	57.1532	60.9315	64.2778	96.5782	101.879	106.629	112.3
90	59.1963	61.7541	65.6466	69.1260	73.2912	107.565	113.145	118.136	124.1
100	67.3276	70.0648	74.2219	77.9295	82.3581	118.498	124.342	129.561	135.8

though, that it only gives an indication and should be used in conjunction with other information to make a decision. You should also bear in mind that the test becomes less reliable as the data sizes become smaller.

SINGLE PERSON DEVIATIONS

Another circumstance that can cause uncertainty is when we find that one person's measurements differ significantly from the rest. This represents the biggest disadvantage in my espoused aim of anonymity in all measurements. By its nature, continuous monitoring does not permit traceability back to an individual. But how frustrating it can be when we discover that one person in our surveyed sample has strong feelings that differ from the rest of the group, yet are unable to talk to them about it or take any action to directly improve their situation.

In such circumstances, there are only three possible courses of action that I have followed:

1. Include the measurement in the calculations and reports, but otherwise do nothing about it.
2. If the survey or interview was conducted by an independent expert who can retain objectivity and anonymity, they can be asked to contact the respondent again and attempt to deal with it.
3. Management can make it known that they are aware that grievances exist and invite anybody who would like to take up the issues raised to make themselves known.

Option 1 is easy but has the obvious disadvantage that the person concerned might feel ignored. However, especially in a large organization, managers may legitimately choose to ignore a single maverick in order to concentrate on the larger picture. I am not keen on the second option since it is still almost impossible to take directly appropriate action without knowing the person's identity. Option 3 can work, if it is felt that this is the right thing to do (bearing in mind that such individual attention can set precedents and cause resentment) as long as it is clearly understood that the exercise will be conducted in a positive manner and the person is not being asked to reveal themselves in order to be disciplined.

In most measurement programmes in which I have been involved, single sets of data from one person that differ widely from the rest are not given any special attention. Although the individual concerned may feel that their views are not being heard, this is usually more than compensated for by the action taken to address wider concerns.

SUMMARY

- In order to be able to appreciate what measurements mean, we have to understand the background to them.
- Measurements and the factors on which they are based are prone to short- and long-term variations.
- A regime needs to be applied to track those environmental factors that have a regular impact on what we do.
- Lagging indicators show what happened but do not reveal it until later – often much later.
- Leading indicators can be used to attempt to predict future trends.
- Slow changes can only be identified by a well-timed measurement regime but are very important.
- Rapid changes are difficult to spot and are often only temporary.
- Trends represent something that needs to be addressed, either to ensure that a good trend continues or that an adverse trend is corrected.
- Short-term deviations ('blips') need to be understood, but should not be a trigger for immediate action without careful thought.
- Similarly, single measurements or sets of results that vary from the expected should be carefully considered to determine what they mean and whether action is appropriate.

CHAPTER ELEVEN

Keeping it Going

INTRODUCTION

I am aware that it upsets many business leaders to be told that they have to stick with something for a long time before any positive results can be seen. In a modern environment, where change is rapid and ever-present, committing to a long-term programme seems incompatible with dynamism and flexibility. There is also much pressure on managers and professionals to produce quick results; nowadays consumer products often have a sales longevity of less than a year before they are replaced by a new model, and commercial pressures are such that finance directors become agitated if capital expenditure does not demonstrate ever-decreasing payback periods.

The problem with all of this is that there is no such thing as a quick fix. Whilst it is true that we have to be able to act quickly and constantly adapt and improve our ways of working, we also have to understand that something that is a sensible business philosophy today will remain a sensible business philosophy for the foreseeable future – procedures and techniques might change rapidly but the fundamentals are less transitory. Most importantly, we have to understand that the real benefits from a programme such as measuring our people can only come through persistence. After all, just setting the systems up will take some time, after which we will need to iron out the inevitable wrinkles in our early efforts, followed by the time needed to obtain an understanding of the levels and meaning of our measurements. We cannot, therefore, drop the programme after only a few weeks and hope that it has done its job; we must assume that what we are introducing will become a permanent feature of the organization; fields seeded now will only produce their full crops after several seasons of nurturing.

This is not to say that our measurement programme will not change. As our systems, processes, products and services develop so must our people, and therefore so must the measurements that we use to monitor them. An organization that is serious about people measurement will continually update its measurements to add new ones, change what is being measured and find new and better ways of using the data. What will be constant, though, is the overall intention and aim to keep track of what is happening with its people.

Our exploration of the subject of people measurement has already taught us that the data gathered is not absolute and is meaningful only by comparison. To conduct such a comparison usually requires at least three sets of data since analysis of only two sets cannot distinguish between, for example, a true trend and a blip. If we are trying to measure feelings, though, with questionnaires or interviews, the sheer effort and scale of such exercises means that collection and analysis of three sets of data will occupy a period of months rather than weeks. Thus even to have one valid point at which action can legitimately be determined may require, including design and planning time, a year-long programme. A permanent, continuing initiative would take even longer to become truly embedded in the corporate culture.

OBJECTIVITY

KEEPING IT STRAIGHT

A key success factor for the long term is to ensure maximum objectivity all the way through the measurement programme, from inception to maturity. It should, of course, be obvious that objectivity is important; after all, the main reason for measuring is so to prevent us from jumping to unfounded and incorrect conclusions about the workforce. Certainly at the beginning of the programme most organizations seem to take reasonable steps to ensure that the measurement results rely as much on objective data as possible. In the longer term, however, it is tempting for short-cuts to be taken – after all, the hard work in setting up the programme was supposed to take place at the outset, and later efforts seem to be hardly worth it when we 'know' what the answer is.

Part of the regular programme should be not only to look at results and attendant actions but also to see where the high ideals of the early days have slipped. A major threat to the long-term sustainability of this type of programme is losing sight of the original objectives and motives for launching it in the first place. Once the whole thing becomes watered down it is an easy step to decide that it is no longer useful or interesting and stop it altogether, wasting the effort that was invested at the beginning.

This is a danger from both sides. The managers who spend time and effort running the measurements, reviewing the outputs and taking actions will become disillusioned if they believe that the sharp edges of the original scheme have been blunted. Similarly, the people being measured will lose faith in it if they see the ideals upon which the programme was sold to them being ignored. Objectivity and fairness are perhaps the most important of these ideals. Any suspicion that personal interest or prejudices are creeping into the measurements will quickly turn people against the process, thus making it difficult to operate and producing less than valuable results.

Constant and open communication is, again, the key here. Planned changes must be discussed widely and the measurement team should meet regularly to review the operation of the programme as well as to deal with issues highlighted by the measurements themselves. It is tempting to drop such meetings once the scheme is mature and running but, without continued energy and discussion, it may well fade and objectivity will certainly be a casualty. Keeping these discussions frank and open is also vital. Subjectivity is most likely to creep in from one or more people administering the measurements, so the opportunity must exist for others to challenge that subjectivity. This in turn can only happen in an honest, open communication framework.

BRANCHING OUT

If objectivity means not letting the scheme become overdominated by the wishes and interests of any individual or group, then this is an appropriate place to discuss the central control of people measurements. General measurements programmes usually permit, even encourage, individual teams and groups to establish and run their own measurements. One of the earliest exponents of operational measurements, Dr W. Edward Deming (whose provenance is mentioned later in this chapter) positively believed that daily measurements should be taken and used by the workers themselves.

People measurements are, however, a little different. When the measurements are product- or process-based, we can simply teach teams how to use measurements well and then let them get on with it. The people element, however, makes this less of an obvious thing to do, for two principal reasons:

- We will usually need to measure all our people in order to obtain a true picture. Although we may wish to distinguish between one group or team and another, this needs to be judged as part of the overall picture to make it possible to identify scales and baselines for the data.
- There are sensitive issues involved. I have, throughout this book, emphasized that measuring people is not like measuring things or processes – feelings and reactions will have to be taken into account. This is best done by a carefully selected and motivated team; there are risks in allowing individual managers to start taking people measurements on their own account.

Although it sounds like the opposite advice to that given for almost any other business performance initiative, in this case I recommend that measuring people remains a centrally driven and controlled activity. This enables some consistency and continuity to be applied while minimizing the risk of adverse reactions from those being measured.

CREATING RIGOUR

IN THE BEGINNING

In the early days, the enthusiasm of those involved in a new project should ensure that a people measurement programme gains and maintains the momentum that it needs. After all, somebody must have had some enthusiasm for it, otherwise it would never have begun in the first place. Creating and introducing the programme will require the design and implementation teams to learn, think in new ways, experiment, adapt their ideas, assess their failures and successes and fine-tune the whole thing to the extent that there should be little opportunity for foot-dragging or lack of energy.

In fact, the biggest problem in creating rigour in the early days is to keep in check some of the enthusiasm and eagerness to get things under way, ensuring instead that things are done in a measured and thought-out manner – for example, by using many of the tools and tips mentioned in this book. Some of this enthusiasm should be channelled into creating a definitive framework and procedure for running the measurement programme. This might perhaps be achieved by selecting a member of the team who has a particular bent for rules and rigour, or even by deliberately appointing such a person to the team if such an aptitude does not already exist amongst the chosen players.

In fact, it is a good idea to be aware of the individual separate skill strengths of all the team members. The same general, well-understood rules for team selection and dynamics that are applied to work and project teams should also apply here. This means that those selecting the champion and review team members should not appoint people simply because they are well liked and share the values and attitudes of the appointment committee. Studies and experience show that the best performing teams are those which contain a mix of skills, preferences and attitudes, as illustrated by the work of the popular Dr Meredith R. Belbin.[1] Any team established to consider the results of measurements and take appropriate action must also be balanced to include both enthusiasm and caution, speed and carefulness, the broad picture and attention to detail. The programme may founder without some hard drivers in the team, but it will also fail if it does not have some careful analysts who wish to ensure that things are done completely and correctly. The rigour that the team will apply will be low from the start if, as is so tempting, everybody appointed to it is an ideas person with no completers/finishers.

---

1. *Team Roles at Work* by M.R. Belbin, London: Butterworth-Heinemann, 1995.

> **TIP**
> Use a recognized team profiling technique, such as that created by Dr
> Belbin, to ensure that you understand the way in which the
> measurement team members will each contribute to the task in hand.

IN THE MEDIUM TERM

Being rigorous is perhaps easiest in the medium term. We are past the initial high-activity phase and so have the experience and time to do things properly. On the other hand, we have not been working at the same thing for so long that it has become too familiar. The key to rigour here is to define the values, policies, guidelines and procedures so that the team know what to do and how to do it. In this way, a consistent and meaningful approach to the measurements can be maintained.

We have already discussed this need in Chapter Ten, but it is important to note the order in which the four requirements above are listed. Procedures – those rules defining exactly how to perform a task or operation – are listed last whereas values, representing what we believe in, come first. The most important factor in keeping the whole team pulling together is not to give them common rules but to ensure that they all believe in the same things. Thus if we can instil in our team the understanding that measurement is valuable, that measurement should not invade individual privacy or attach blame, that personal dignity is important and that doing things well is more important than doing them cheaply or quickly, this will have a greater impact upon team cohesion and direction than ensuring that everybody always records their actions on a form 37B. Policies represent the way in which values directly relate to how our business is run and guidelines give information on how the team should react to situations, so that, together, the four requirements represent the transition from general principles to specific instructions.

This is not to say that standard procedures and instructions are not important; we need to have a high degree of standardization to make the whole project work. The problem is that there are always cases where the procedures do not quite apply, or which are exceptions to the rule. In such cases, we need to understand the wider values of the organization and the measurement programme to know how to react to those exceptions and grey areas.

IN THE LONG TERM

The danger in the long term is simply a loss of interest or complacency. Devotion to, and belief in, a new project is easy when it is fresh and sparkly but can quickly wane with time. After a while it can even turn into an irritating chore. If this happens to any significant degree the signs quickly become obvious so that everybody loses faith in the programme. There is also the danger, of course, that people become less rigorous in their use of the measurements so that their value is reduced.

It might seem to some that such decay is not really a long-term risk. After all, all organizations have stable and relatively routine operations such as order processing, invoice payment and credit control that do not suffer from reducing effectiveness and consistency over time. The reason for this is the very ordinariness of the work. These tasks continue to be done well and diligently because they are seen as mainstream. The trick, then, is to make people measurement seem just as ordinary as other activities. Although I have often referred to 'the measurement project' or 'the measurement programme', in fact the whole exercise should be managed and publicized in a way that encourages everyone to understand that keeping track of our people via quantitative techniques is a core part of the way in which we will be running our business from now on – not something tacked on to the side that will eventually be dropped when we become bored with it.

While making the measurements central and mainstream is key to keeping them alive and maintaining an appropriate level of rigour, there are also some other things that can be done to keep interest and involvement high:

- Rotate members of the measurement analysis and action team (and the champion, if appropriate) to ensure a constant supply of fresh blood.
- Find new measurements that will create renewed interest, and drop old ones that no longer have as much use or meaning.
- Set increased targets for those areas that are already performing well and challenge people to find a way of meeting them.
- Find new ways of presenting the data so that the displays and reports do not look dated and stale.

CONSTANCY OF PURPOSE

ORIGINS OF THE PHRASE

Dr W. Edward Deming is one of the people credited with founding and defining the quality revolution, and particularly with acting as a catalyst for the remarkable manufacturing growth of post-war Japan. Dr Deming was an academic who rejected some of the old aspects of 'scientific management' and Taylorism which argued that efficiency was created by breaking work down into small components and giving people repetitive single tasks to complete so that there would be limited room for error. He espoused an alternative approach in which management, not workers, was responsible for the majority of errors and where workers should be provided with the training, tools and flexibility to contribute to quality and eliminate errors. Together with a few contemporaries, he visited Japan where his ideas generated great enthusiasm in a country that had to try to compete on the world stage yet had far fewer resources than were available to its competitors in the West, especially the USA.

Deming's teaching is often said to be encompassed by his '14 points' which lay out the fundamental principles for transforming quality within an organization. These provided the foundation for many total quality management (TQM) initiatives adopted worldwide in all forms of company and operation. Although the popularity of total quality management as a business programme has waned, this has as much to do with the fact that it was so successful that most of the principles have now become mainstream, rather than any fundamental failing or weakness of the philosophy itself.

One of Deming's 14 points was 'constancy of purpose'. He argued that TQM could only work if those at the very top of the company (a familiar theme) were not only committed to the ideas but also accepted that they were in it for the long term and would not lose heart at the first hurdle or when improvements failed to arrive as quickly as hoped.

STICKING TO YOUR GUNS

This same applies to people measurement. It is not an improvement method designed to give quick paybacks and instant gratification. This is, of course, a point in its favour since most experienced managers express significant mistrust in 'quick fixes' – the derogatory comments often made, today, about business process re-engineering (a tool of the 1980s that promised quick and substantial process improvements and cost savings) is just one example.

However, a consequence of this is that everyone must be ready to provide long-term commitment in order to see any benefits. Intellectually, this is not so hard to do at the outset of the project. After all, we all understand that anything worth having is worth working for so we know that we will have to work for it and keep at it. What is more difficult, though, is to maintain that commitment when the programme is already several months old, has cost the company money, has perhaps addressed some employee concerns but is still treated by them with a little suspicion and still requires significant effort to develop. It is even trickier if something else of an apparent higher priority crops up, such as the loss of a major contract or – even harder to deal with – the winning of a major contract. Under such circumstances it is tempting to argue that, whilst people measurement was a good idea at the time, circumstances have now changed and it is not worth pursuing. Whilst it is recognized that very occasionally circumstances change to such an extent that the programme as designed is no longer appropriate (head office policy changes that cause the loss of two-thirds of our workforce, for example), in most cases we must stick to what we intended and ride out any short-term distractions in order to gain the full benefit from what we have done. To do otherwise is to waste all the effort put in during the early stages. So when managers say at the outset that they are committed for the long term, it must be made quite clear to them that they really must mean it and that they cannot afford to be diverted at the first hurdle.

COMBINING WITH OTHER PROGRAMMES

In many 'support' fields (that is, specializations such as personnel, quality, information technology, facilities, finance and so on that only indirectly contribute to principal operations) there is regular debate about the merits, or otherwise, of integration with other support functions. For example, since financial tasks lend themselves extraordinarily well to the number-crunching abilities of computer systems, information technology responsibilities often lie with the finance manager in small to medium-sized enterprises, or the responsibilities for umbrella quality and health and safety management are often allocated to the same person. In such cases, it is often argued that one discipline is diluted, or weakened, by having to cope with the demands of the other.

In terms of combining a people measurement programme with other initiatives this argument has a mixed perspective, depending on the viewpoint being applied. One common reaction is to worry that our aims will be diluted. As we now know, directly measuring people differs from other measurement processes in terms of the sensitivity and care that needs to be applied. Other initiatives may not include, or have the need for, such sensitivity and could therefore jeopardize the patient work that we have put into measuring people well and effectively. For instance, using the same teams, tools and techniques as the product quality measurement programme could lead to confusion between absolute measurements (as most product measurements will be) and the relative measurements associated with people monitoring. Or even worse, tying the type of measurements considered in this book into a personal objective and appraisal system, would bring into conflict the ideas of zero blame and a sampling approach with the more individually focused aims of an appraisal system.

Many of these arguments, however, miss the point. Any initiative that is seen as something separate to the rest of the business will at best have limited benefit and at worst will actually hinder efficiency, effectiveness and progress. Examples of the latter case include many badly managed certification and award programmes, where the leadership of the organization is so keen to possess the appropriate official recognition that they are willing to suffer procedures and disciplines that take efficiency away from the main operation for no other purpose than to satisfy the external evaluator. In such cases, the activities needed to meet the standards of the award are treated as something extra to what the organization 'normally' does rather than an integral part of it, and they often do enough damage to counteract the benefits gained by the award. An example of this is the popular view that some of the early Malcolm Baldridge Quality Award winners in the USA found themselves in financial difficulties from the effort that they had to expend to fulfil their obligations as publicly acknowledged award winners.

No initiative by management for the good of the organization should suffer this fate. Each should have benefits that enhance the overall operations, and the best way of doing this, as already discussed when dealing with how to maintain rigour, is to make it part of normal operations. If everybody views what we are doing as an essential element of business, rather than an irritating extra task generated by the latest fashionable scheme, then the whole operation is far more likely to be successful. A common example with which some readers may be familiar is the discussion of whether or not to combine quality management systems with those applied for dealing with health and safety. Of course they should; the way in which we control the issue of documents or define best operating practice should be the corporate way – if users are likely to find multiple schemes annoying or confusing and will ignore them.

In this light, of course, the measurement programme should be integrated with other activities because it should all be combined with other activities as an integrated whole; discussions of which programmes should be combined is therefore irrelevant since they should all be made to behave as part of a single system. Measuring how people are behaving and feeling should quickly become a standard part of what we do at work.

This is not to say that everything has to be standardized to a ridiculous degree or be controlled by exactly the same people. In an organization it is quite normal to set up a special team to deal with a new contract bid, or to handle a development project. We can do the same for our measurement programme, as long as the team is perceived as doing something that is a logical part of what we do rather than a sideline.

MAINTAINING THE MOMENTUM

If we follow the philosophy that measuring people should be integrated into normal operations then keeping up the momentum is no longer an issue; it should become as natural as dealing with the monthly payroll which nobody considers may decline because the payroll department staff become bored with it. A parallel of how this can work is found in computer system back-up – in the early days of desktop computer usage, back-up was something that only security enthusiasts worried about, but it was quickly realized that it was an important activity and, in most organizations, it has now become a routine daily task that is carried out without question. Although a people measurement programme is more complex than this, much of the data collection and reporting is straightforward and can be made part of standard daily tasks.

Of course, there are questions of how we maintain the interest and enthusiasm of people generally. Any group of employees can suffer a loss of morale or interest, whatever the activities in which they are involved. The good thing is that with an integrated approach, where people measurement is just part of the way in which we manage the business, then maintaining high morale can be addressed in the tried and tested ways that managers have always learnt and most organizational leaders continue to pursue.

Finally, the main things that will help to maintain the momentum is running the programme well and producing results that are worthwhile for both employees and the organization. In this way everybody will benefit and should thus wish to keep it going.

SUMMARY

- It is important to keep the programme going long enough to see benefits, despite pressures for quick results.
- Allowing the measurement programme to change and develop will assist its longevity.
- Objectivity in the long term is one key to effectiveness.
- Communication from all sides will encourage long-term support from everybody.
- Central coordination enables common standards to be applied and mistakes to be avoided.
- At the start of the project, a mixed and balanced team needs to be created in order to avoid excesses in any direction.
- The team should be supported and driven by a carefully defined set of values, policies and procedures.
- Measuring people should gradually become part of normal business; this will help maintain momentum and avoid the danger of it being perceived as secondary to routine operations.
- Managers must be fully prepared to commit to the programme for the long term – a measurement programme cannot provide a quick fix.
- Real commitment and long-term momentum will arise from the results being used well and leading to worthwhile actions.

Index

absolute targets 111–12
acceptability as a measurement criterion 43
accountancy practices 120–21
action
    areas for 114–18
    monitoring of 122–3
action planning 119–22
analysis of results
    from continuous monitoring 102–3
    from employee surveys 68–74
    from interview programmes 87–92
anonymity in surveys 64–5, 73, 135
appraisal of personal performance 12–13, 27, 30, 141
availability of results from measurement 32, 43, 103–5
average values 68

bar charts 70–73
baselining 108–11, 123
behaviour
    as distinct from feelings 36–7, 114
    hierarchies of 38
    interlinkages in 37–8
Belbin, M.R. 138–9
benchmarking 54
benchmarking surveys 110
'big picture', the 22
'blips' 117–18, 131–5
body language 53
brainstorming 97, 119–20
business process re-engineering 8, 140–41

calibration of measurements 56, 59, 78
certification programmes 141–2
'champions' 107–9, 119
change, coping with 3–4
change programmes, need for 52
chi-square tests 133–4
'churn' of products 1
committees to oversee measurement 57;
    see also teams for reviewing measurement
    programme reports
communication with employees 32, 101–2, 137, 143
competition 1
conditions of employment 16
constancy of purpose 140–41
consultants, use of 67, 76, 84, 110–11

continuous monitoring 51, 94–106, 114–15, 123
    advantages and disadvantages of 94–5, 105
    analysis of results 102–3
    design of 96–8
    planning and preparation for 98–102, 105
    procedures for 102
    reporting on 103
    reviewing of systems for 105–6
conversational style of interviewing 85–6
cost–benefit comparisons 120–21
customer expectations 5–6
customer satisfaction 4, 40, 44
customer satisfaction surveys 49–50
cyclic effects 132–3

data collection 102
    on environmental factors 127
degrees of freedom 133
Deming, W.E. 137, 140
direct and indirect measurement 12, 52–3, 58
diversity
    in measurement 28
    of viewpoints 27–8, 33
dual targets 112–13

emotions, taking account of 26, 126
employee surveys 5, 50, 59–75
    analysis of results 68–74
    cost of 66–7
    coverage of 63–4
    quality of 65–6
    timing of 59
environmental factors 125–7, 132–3
evaluation criteria 46–9
expectations
    of customers 5–6
    of employees 35

'failure modes and effects' analysis 121
feelings
    as distinct from behaviours 36–7, 114
    recognition of 23–6, 31–3
financial measurement 39–40, 44
forms, use of 101
foundation element of success in business 16
fuelling element of success in business 16–17

Gantt charts 68
gaps between actual and desired performance
    62–3, 68, 110, 114–15
genetic technology 2

'happy sheets' 48–9
hours of work 16
human contribution to business activity 15–18;
    see also people, importance of

immediate availability of results 43
importance of issues to survey respondents 62
importance of tasks *versus* their urgency 21
impressions, making constructive use of 28–31
indirect actions 128
indirect indicators 51–3, 58, 129
individual data in reports 104–6
individual deviations 135
individuality 26–7, 33
integrity 33
internal customers 39
Internet, the, use of 116
Internet service providers 2
interviews as a means of measurement 50–51,
    76–83
    analysis of results 87–92
    conduct of 83–7
    duration of 80–81
    for obtaining baseline data 110–11
    planning of 77–9
    questions put in 81–3
    reporting on results from 90–92
    strengths and weaknesses of 92–3
    timing of 79–81
intuition 22–6 *passim*, 46
Investors in People 63
ISO 9001 standard 39–40

Japanese production methods 1, 140
justification of conclusions 31

key success factors 19–21

lagging indicators 127–9, 135
leading indicators 129, 135
lighting-level studies 42
Lock, Dennis 68
long-term problems 126
loyalty 35, 38, 113–14, 119–20
lunch breaks 129–30

Malcolm Baldridge Quality Award winners 142
management by objectives 17
manipulation of data 55, 57
manuals 28
'mean and range' approach to measurement
    13–14
mean values 68; *see also* moving averages
measurement
    choice of subjects for 34–44, 96–8
    limits to usefulness of 131
    negative effects of 42–3
    pitfalls in 54–8

measurement continuum 8–9, 41, 44
measurement criteria 43–4
median values 68–9
medical information 33, 52–3
millennium bug 20–21
mission statements 7
modal values 68–9
Monarch of the Glen 6
monitoring
    of action following from measurement
        122–3
    advantages and disadvantages of 94–5
    of change generally 4
    constructiveness in use of 30–31
    methods of 100–101
    see also continuous monitoring
morale 31–2, 40, 114–15, 126–8, 142
motorcycle industry 1
moving averages 14, 116

'noise' in results 117
normal distribution 71–2
norms for an industry 111
'not applicable' options in questionnaires 61
nuclear generation of electricity 2

objectives
    of business activity 6–7, 51–2, 96
    of recruitment 25
objectivity 24, 29, 33, 46–7, 137–8, 143
observer effects 42–3
one-off occurrences 127
openness, culture of 32–3, 103
opinions, monitoring of 101
options for action 119–20
organizational influences on business activity
    18–19
output measurement 17

people, importance of 11–12
people measurement
    as core part of business process 140
    characteristics of 9–12, 22, 41, 52, 137–8, 141
    differences from measurement of processes
        38
    integration with other activities 141–3
people success factors 20
personal reaction, levels of 13–15
prediction of future problems 129
prejudice 24
presentations on results of measurement 92
primary concerns 20–21
priorities of management and of staff 114–15,
    123
problem-solving methods 119
process measurement 4–5, 38–9
process thinking 13
profit, measurement of 40–41

project management and project planning 68, 122
psychological profiling 62
publication of results of evaluations 32

quality audits 28
quality management 18, 142
quantification and quantifiability 43, 53–4
questionnaires 49–51
questions
    in employee surveys 59–62
    in interviews 81–3

ranges of measurements 69–72
rapid changes 130–31, 135
recommendations in reports 90
recording of interviews 86
recruitment
    of individual members of staff 24–5
    of teams 27, 138–9, 143
religion 36
repeatability of measurements and evaluations 31, 47
reports
    on continuous monitoring 103–4
    on interview projects 90–92
representativeness as a measurement criterion 43
review of measurement programme reports 107–9
rigour in measurement 138–40
risk analysis 121

sampling for monitoring purposes 98–9
satisfaction sheets 48–9
scales, definition of 46–9, 54, 58, 129–30
scientific approach to measurement 31
'scientific management' 140
scoring systems 47, 89
second-party assessment 50–51, 76
secret monitoring 104, 106
self-assessment 49–50
service industries 2
sexual harassment 17

short-term problems 126
sign-based measurement 51
significance testing 133
slow changes 129–30, 135
spread, measures of 14, 69–72
spreadsheets, use of 74, 115–16
stability as a measurement criterion 44
standard deviation 14–15, 70–72
standard procedures 139
statistical techniques 116; *see also* significance testing; standard deviation
strategies 6
strength of responses to questions 89–90
stress for employees 128–9
support for employees 6, 18
surveys *see* customer satisfaction surveys; employee surveys
suspicion on the part of the workforce 31
systems approaches 13

target-setting 54–5, 111–13, 123
Taylorism 140
teams
    for reviewing measurement programme reports 107–9
    selection of members for 27, 138–9, 143
time-lags 127–9
timeliness of reporting 103
total quality management 15, 56, 140
trends 132–5
trust 16–17, 33, 105, 120

uncertainty
    dealing with 8
    measurement of 45–6
understandability as a measurement criterion 43
urgency of tasks *versus* their importance 21

variance 133

working environment 18

Y2K problem 20–21